GROWING
CHURCHES,

GROWING
LEADERS

How to Lead a Growing Church
and Live a Balanced Life

DAVID FAUST

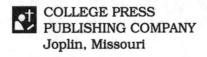

COLLEGE PRESS
PUBLISHING COMPANY
Joplin, Missouri

To my wife Candy,
my treasured
grace-giver, burden-sharer,
and friend.

ACKNOWLEDGMENTS

Thanks to my prayer-group friends who frequently lifted me, and this book, before God's throne of grace; to Wendi Breese, Judy Pratt, and Trena Lieb for their help in typing the manuscript; and to my wife and children for graciously understanding the difficulty of keeping my own life in balance while writing a book on balanced living.

A few portions of this book appeared first as articles in *Christian Standard* and *Lookout* magazines. Chapter Nine also includes material from my article, "Overcoming the Lone Ranger Syndrome," which appeared in the February, 1994, edition of *Church Administration*.

Finally, special thanks to my coworkers and students at Cincinnati Bible College & Seminary and the congregations at South Nassau and University Christian Church who have helped me grow as a man and as a minister. May the Lord keep all of us growing gracefully.

TABLE OF CONTENTS

INTRODUCTION

Before I wrote this book, I lived it.

My life as a church leader has not been a picnic. But come to think of it, at times it has resembled a *circus*.

I have often felt like a trapeze artist, moving fast and hanging on for dear life. I have learned to be a juggler, alternately handling the diverse roles of husband, father, preacher, teacher, and writer. Encountering a few problem people has increased my appreciation for lion tamers. But most of the time, this circus we call ministry has made me feel like a tightrope walker, for a big part of success is in keeping your balance.

I joined the ministry circus at an early age. I grew up in a Christian home, and my dad served as an elder in our church. Ordained in my early twenties, I have served on the staff of three churches, including a ten-year preaching ministry in New York and a church-planting role with the congregation where I presently serve part-time in Cincinnati while teaching full-time in a Bible college.

Over the years, I have experienced firsthand the difficult dilemma many church leaders face. Dedicated men and women devote ever-increasing time and energy to their ministries; but in the process, they often find themselves living unbalanced lives. Their goals may be noble and their motives pure, but the long hours and hard work required to grow a church can take a heavy toll. A blazing pace replaces amazing grace.

In the early years of my own ministry, I especially felt a tension between my *family* responsibilities and my *church* responsibilities. Whenever I diligently pursued the work of the ministry, I was plagued by a guilty conscience which nagged, "You should be spending more time with your family." On the other hand, when I felt I was spending ample time with my wife and three children, I was haunted by the awareness that there were so many lost sheep to be found, fed, and shepherded.

Further, as I worked with a growing number of seekers and new Christians, I noticed that the problems real people face do not always fit neatly into the tight theological categories I had learned in the church and the seminary. Since I was firmly committed to the inspiration and authority of Scripture, I did not want to compromise any sound principle of Biblical theology, but again, I recognized the need for balance. Convinced that *fulfilling Christ's Great Commission* **is** *sound theology*, I was determined to present an authentic and understandable gospel to real people who struggle to find meaning in today's world.

While studying in the Doctor of Ministry program at Fuller Theological Seminary, I observed these same tensions among many of my fellow students. I attended exciting classes in church growth where professors like C. Peter Wagner encouraged us to be pragmatic and fearless, sparing no cost in reaching a lost world for Christ. But I also took a fascinating course called "The Minister's Personal Growth," in which Archibald Hart challenged us to lead balanced lives of emotional and spiritual wholeness. Both perspectives were inspirational and helpful, but at times, they almost seemed contradictory.

Is it really possible to lead a growing church while also leading a balanced life? While writing this book, I have spoken with numerous friends and colleagues who excitedly affirm the need for someone to address this topic. At the same time, many express doubts about the possibility of achieving a true balance.

My friends hear the same divergent voices which have clamored for my attention throughout my ministry. Church growth practitioners urge us to lead boldly, work tirelessly, and give of ourselves sacrificially. Pastoral counselors advise us to take care of ourselves and our families. Spiritual mentors exhort us to be people of holiness and prayer. Theologians warn us to be faithful to the Scripture, never compromising the truth in order to make ourselves more comfortable or the gospel more palatable.

If ministry were a multiple-choice test, it seems we are forced to choose just one of the following options:

A. Be a dynamic leader in a growing church, devoting ourselves to the ministry.

B. Be an attentive and available spouse and parent, devoting ourselves to the family.

C. Be a healthy person, physically fit and spiritually deep, devoting ourselves to a personal relationship with God.

Some leaders feel compelled to select and pursue one of these options at all costs. Others, overcome with frustration, simply opt for "None of the Above" and experience a certain level of despair at their personal and pastoral mediocrity.

The idea I want to present in this book, however, is that the best option is "All of the Above." It is not only desirable, but possible, to pursue church growth while maintaining our theological integrity and personal health. It is possible to find a healthy balance which harmonizes such issues as:

(1) Combining *church* growth with *personal* growth;

(2) Devoting oneself to *commitment* and *responsibility*,

11

while also experiencing *contentment* and *rest*;

(3) Striving for *success*, while learning to deal with the reality of *failure*;

(4) Achieving desired *results*, while maintaining a *Biblical perspective*.

These are difficult but resolveable matters. The answer is not to choose church growth at the cost of one's personal health, nor the reverse. Certainly the answer is not to be found in theological compromise. The only solution is to GROW GRACEFULLY, depending more completely upon the grace of God in our lives as individuals and as congregations.

God's grace offers encouraging, practical help for leaders who want their churches to grow, but are also concerned about personal wholeness for themselves and their church's members.

To address these needs, I have divided this book into two major sections. Part One, "The Graceful Church," argues for a grace-centered (rather than performance-centered) approach to evangelism and edification. In the process of presenting a theological rationale for growing gracefully, I present a friendly critique of certain excesses in the church growth movement which may contribute to a lack of balance. Part Two, "The Graceful Leader," deals with many of the personal issues facing leaders and their families today.

This book is the product of a twofold burden God has laid upon my heart: (1) a burden for the church to reach her full potential in reaching the lost and building up the saved, and (2) a burden for the leaders who sacrificially lay down their lives every day so the church can reach that potential. Since I bear some scars of my own received in the battle for balance, I write not from the comfortable position of a detached observer, but from the perspective of an understanding co-laborer.

I encourage my readers to join me in the daily, lifelong process of growing gracefully.

> But grow in the grace and knowledge of our Lord and Savior Jesus Christ. To him be glory both now and forever! Amen (2 Pet 3:18).

PART ONE:

THE GRACEFUL CHURCH

1
GOD'S GRACE-GIVERS

Graceful is a beautiful word.

Gracefulness brings to mind the agility of great athletes: a strong-limbed swimmer gliding effortlessly through the water, a sure-footed figure skater spinning flawlessly on the ice, an acrobatic wide receiver catching the football while keeping both feet inbounds.

Gracefulness also brings to mind the social gentility of a gracious hostess who makes visitors feel welcome in her home. And the dignified touch of a great musician who expresses a song with technical precision and emotional power.

But, most importantly, gracefulness is a spiritual quality.

Think of it: *grace-fullness!* The word implies more than a mere taste of grace. It suggests instead the kind of full and satisfying awareness of God's blessings which led David to say, "My cup overflows" (Ps 23:5). It beckons us to drink deeply of God's unmerited mercy and experience the liberating joy of forgiveness.

The apostle Paul never tired of describing (though he termed it indescribable) the "surpassing grace" God has given His people (2 Cor 9:14-15). Paul wanted nothing more than to know Christ, preach Christ, and eventually to be with Christ. He planted churches with unflinching zeal because he was totally captivated by the grace of God. Paul was a man of many talents and many accomplishments. "But by the grace of God," he wrote, "I am what I am" (1 Cor 15:10).

Grace is one of the most precious concepts in the Bible, for it expresses the essence of the gospel: the good news of God's redeeming love. Grace is *free* — it is an undeserved and unearned gift. It is also *freeing*, for graceful people escape the enslaving viewpoint which insists that serving God always means trying harder and doing more.

Tragically, though, many churches fail to teach and preach grace. Cheri, a young woman brought up in a Bible-believing church, cannot remember ever hearing a sermon or lesson on grace. "We heard a lot about what we should do to please God," she recalls, "but very little about what God has done for us."

Cheri's sad story is not unusual. As a teacher in a Christian college, I have encountered numerous young people who have been reared in Christian homes, and who have attended Sunday School and worship services every week for years, but possess almost no concept of the marvel of God's grace.

Church life produces pressures which only compound the problem. As leaders, we feel the pressure to perform, to produce, to prove our own worth by accomplishing enormous amounts of work. We become skillful schedule jugglers, and earn the admiration of people impressed by our busy lives and our ability to get things done. At the same time, however, we often sense a certain grace-void in our lives. We find it difficult to slow down enough to give and receive grace.

Too often, God's call to be a grace-giver is replaced by the minister's own drive to be a high-achiever.

We seem to think that when God calls us to ministry, He calls *collect* — as if somehow, we are eventually going to have to *pay* for this! God does not call collect; through Christ, He has already paid the price in full.

God *does*, however, place His calls *person-to-person!*

In fact, He has provided two life-sized personal illustrations of what it means to live and grow gracefully.

The first example is Jesus Christ. God's Son is the perfect embodiment of grace. A second illustration may be found in the New Testament church. Jesus transformed ordinary men and women into a band of believers who literally changed the world for good. Like Jesus Himself, these early Christians were God's grace-givers, extending the grace of God to hurting people.

GOD'S GRACE IN THE LIFE OF JESUS

Surprisingly, the word *grace* (Greek *charis*) rarely appears in the four gospels. Matthew and Mark do not use the word at all, and it occurs a mere dozen times in Luke and John combined. The gospel writers record only two occasions in which Jesus used *charis*. One is Luke 6:32-34, where the word is translated "thanks" or "credit": "If you love those who love you, what *credit* [*charis*] is that to you? Even 'sinners' love those who love them. . . ." The other is Luke 17:9, where again the word is used in the general sense of "thanks."

Nevertheless, Jesus frequently illustrated grace in His teachings. His parable of the lost son provides an unforgettable description of the father's gracious love extended to a child who strayed from home (Luke 15:11-32). In Jesus' parable about the Pharisee and the tax collector, the man who humbly admits his sin and appeals to God for mercy goes home justified, not the man who proudly recounts his own good deeds (Luke 18:9-14). While dining at Zacchaeus' house, Jesus affirmed the gracious salvation of this short man with the long list of sins: "Today salvation has come to this house . . . for the Son of Man came to seek and to save what was lost" (Luke 19:9-10).

Most important, Jesus Himself was a living example of grace.

Full of Grace and Truth

The New Testament begins with the tedious-to-read but historically important genealogy of Jesus (Matt 1:1-17). It includes people like the conniving Jacob, the harlot Rahab, the adulterous David (and Uriah's wife, with whom David committed adultery), and the evil Manasseh. Even Jesus' early ancestry reveals God's ability to use less-than-perfect people to accomplish His gracious purpose.

God's angel Gabriel told Jesus' mother, the virgin Mary, that she had found favor or grace with God (Luke 1:30). Jesus grew up in an atmosphere of grace under the supervision of Mary and her righteous husband Joseph. Scripture sums up Jesus' early childhood with these words: "And the child grew and become strong; He was filled with wisdom, and *the grace of God was upon Him*" (Luke 2:40, italics mine).

Later, Luke paints a similar portrait of the period from Jesus' adolescence to His adulthood: "And Jesus grew in wisdom and stature, and in favor [literally, *grace*] with God and men" (Luke 2:52). Even as a young man growing up in Nazareth, Jesus epitomized the well-balanced life. Intellectually, physically, spiritually, and socially, Jesus experienced the full range of human development. Simply stated, He grew gracefully!

When Jesus began His public ministry, His listeners were impressed both by the authority and the graciousness of His teaching. When he visited Nazareth, for example, the people "were amazed at the gracious words that came from His lips" (Luke 4:22). He angered these same listeners, however, when He pointed out how God extended His grace to people living outside of Israel. Sometimes grace is not the message people want to hear. Jesus' graceful teaching nearly resulted in His being thrown down a cliff (Luke 4:28-30).

John's gospel describes the glory of the incarnation by emphasizing the gracefulness of Christ. "The Word became flesh and lived for a while among us. We have seen His glory, the glory of the one and only Son, who came from the Father, *full of grace and truth*" (John 1:14, italics mine). Further, John writes, "From the fullness of His grace we have all received one blessing after another. For the law was given through Moses; *grace and truth came through Jesus Christ*" (John 1:16-17, italics mine).

Out of all the marvelous things it meant for God to send His son to earth, one of the most important is this: Jesus furnished a living illustration of grace.[1]

Bruised Reeds and Smoldering Wicks

To the surprise of His disciples, Jesus dealt gracefully with hurting people. He took the time to engage in a life-changing conversation with a Samaritan woman whose life had been tarnished by having had five husbands (John 4:4-42). He purposely visited the sick who lay near the pool of Bethesda, and healed the most desperate among them: a man who had been an invalid for thirty-eight years (John 5:1-15).

Jesus' priorities were dictated by grace, not by guilt. His ministry focused on the importance of blessing people, not on impressing important people. He touched lepers whom others shunned. He freed the demon-possessed whom others feared. He took time for children whom others shooed away.

Jesus demonstrated the unfettered freedom of a grace-driven life.

He did the unexpected. He surprised everyone by inviting despised tax collectors like Matthew and Zacchaeus to be His disciples, and then demonstrated the accessibility of His grace by dining in their homes (Matt 9:9-10, Luke 19:1-10).

He loved the unrespected. Despite the Pharisees' self-righteous criticism, Jesus openly associated with well-known sinners, reminding everyone, "It is not the healthy who need a doctor, but the sick" (Matt 9:11-12). Like many of today's performance-oriented church leaders, the Pharisees had earned the respect of their contemporaries by their hard work and their many sacrifices. But Jesus instructed them to reexamine their priorities and restudy the Scripture which says God desires mercy, not sacrifice (Matt 9:13, Hos 6:6).

He saved the unperfected. Jesus did not come to call those who prove their own worthiness through personal achievement. He came to call sinners who are poor enough in spirit to recognize their utter dependence on His grace (Matt 9:13, Rom 5:6-8).

Isaiah used an interesting word-picture when he predicted the coming Messiah's work. Prophetically describing the tender way Christ dealt with people, Isaiah wrote: "A bruised reed He will not break, and a smoldering wick He will not snuff out . . . ." (Isa 42:3). Matthew quotes this Scripture when describing Jesus' healing ministry among the sick (Matt 12:15-21).

Bruised reeds and smoldering wicks vividly portray the way many people feel: hurt, burning out, easily crushed, vulnerable. Since reeds are naturally weak, bruising only makes matters worse. Smoldering, smoky candle wicks could easily be snuffed out and destroyed. But Jesus gracefully cared for those who were bruised, broken, and burned out. He labored to restore their strength and rekindle their flame. He came not to condemn, but to save (John 3:17).

My Yoke Is Easy

Jesus manifested His grace in special ways to His

disciples. When their busy lives left them exhausted, He called them away to a quiet place where they could rest (Mark 6:30-31). When their personal ambition led to disputes among themselves, Jesus reminded them of their purpose as servants (Mark 9:33-35). When their hearts were troubled, He reassured them of His love (John 14:1, 15:9). When their minds were filled with doubts, He gave them convincing evidence of His power (Luke 24:36-49).

Jesus called His followers to an absolute, fully-surrendered life of commitment. Still, He called them *gracefully*. He did not say, "Come to me, all you who are strong and driven, and I will give you more work to do." He said, "Come to me, all you who are weary and burdened, and I will give you rest" (Matt 11:28). Jesus realistically warned His disciples that the road of discipleship will be difficult and often filled with pain. But at the same time, He offered sustaining grace for the journey.

Jesus' words in Matthew 11:29-30 are both comforting and a little bewildering: "Take my yoke upon you and learn from me, for I am gentle and humble in heart, and you will find rest for your souls. For my yoke is easy and my burden is light." Many honest believers puzzle over these words, for the Christian life seems anything but easy. Leaders, particularly, carry heavy burdens. Instead of rest for our souls, we find stress, conflicts, and pressures of many kinds.

Part of the answer may be in understanding the meaning of the word "easy" in this passage. The Greek word *chrestos* literally means "kind" or "well-fitting," like a well-crafted ox-yoke that fits smoothly around the animal's neck. An ox must perform hard labor, but a *chrestos* yoke enables him to do his work without chafing. Similarly, Christ expects His servants to work hard, but His purpose is not to make us miserable in the process. He graciously gives His servants well-fitting equipment to ease the burden and lighten the load.

Perhaps another part of the problem is that so many of us do not take *Jesus'* yoke upon ourselves. Instead, we fall under weighty yokes of our own making. We place around our necks the heavy and sometimes unreasonable expectations of others. Thus the burden grows heavier, and our zest for ministry wanes. Church leaders who try too hard to please the crowd soon discover there are always plenty of people around like the Pharisees in Jesus' day who "tie up heavy loads and put them on men's shoulders" (Matt 23:4).

Before the Master said, "Go into all the world and make disciples," He said, "Come to me and I will give you rest." He said, "Learn from me," not "Prove yourself."

The Lord remains full of grace and truth. He has never stopped being a grace-giver. He reaches out to the weary worker who has been losing the bruising battle for balance. His gracious invitation applies not only to the lost soul outside his kingdom, but also to the wounded warrior inside: "Come to me, all you who are weary and burdened, and I will give you rest."

GOD'S GRACE IN THE BOOK OF ACTS

After Jesus ascended back to heaven, His spiritual body, the church, continued "what He began to do and to teach" (Acts 1:1), including a continuing emphasis on God's grace. The phrase, "growing gracefully," typified the life of the disciples, for the church in the book of Acts was both a growing church and a graceful church.

Luke describes the exciting growth of the Antioch church as "evidence of the grace of God" (Acts 11:23).

Paul and Barnabas urged new converts to "continue in the grace of God" (Acts 13:43). Signs and wonders performed by the apostles were done by the power of God to confirm "the message of His grace" (Acts 14:3). Missionary work was accomplished after the messengers were first "committed to the grace of God" (Acts 14:26, 15:40). People were saved "through the grace of our Lord Jesus" (Acts 15:11, 18:27). The preacher's role was "testifying to the gospel of God's grace" (Acts 20:24). Elders were committed "to God and to the word of His grace" (Acts 20:32).

In one short passage, Acts 4:31-33, Luke gives us a glimpse of this graceful church in action. This text reveals five characteristics of a graceful church.

1. Spiritual Vitality

"They were all filled with the Holy Spirit" (Acts 4:31).

I remember hearing about a man who froze to death while sitting on a large chunk of coal. The problem was, he had no concept of the power available to him. Likewise, some churches have a form of godliness but have no concept of the power of God.

The church described in the book of Acts lived and thrived by the power of the Holy Spirit. The secret of church growth was not human achievement, but divine empowerment.

The Holy Spirit does not produce cowards. Graceful churches, filled with spiritual vitality, still speak the word of God boldly. They heed the words of Paul: "Be strong in the Lord and in His mighty power" (Eph 6:10), and the words of John: "The one who is in you is greater than the one who is in the world" (1 John 4:4).

2. Heart-Level Unity

"All the believers were one in heart and mind" (Acts 4:32).

Jesus had prayed for unity (John 17:20-23), and now His followers lived it. Certainly this does not mean they experienced no personality conflicts or differences of opinion. But at least for a period of time, God's people managed to keep such issues from dividing them. Instead, they focused on the centrality of Christ and a united vision for His work.

These graceful Christians experienced firsthand the blessed condition David envisioned in Psalm 133:1: "How good and pleasant it is when brothers live together in unity!" It was the powerful kind of bond in which those who call on the name of the Lord "serve Him shoulder to shoulder" (Zeph 3:9).

J. W. McGarvey described this heart-level unity as follows:

> Considering the large number of persons in this congregation, and the variety of social relations from which they had been suddenly drawn together, it is truly remarkable, and well worthy of a place in the record, that they were "of one heart and soul." The unity for which the Saviour had prayed was now enjoyed by the church, and witnessed by the world. The most surprising manifestation of it was seen in that complete lack of selfishness which led one and all to say that the things which he possessed were not his own, but the property of all. This was not the result of socialistic theorizing, or of rules laid down to govern all who sought admission into the new society; but it was the spontaneous expression of the love of God and man which had taken possession of every heart.[2]

Imperfect people cannot be united without grace. In working with churches over the years, I have observed that *mistakes* usually do not destroy relationships. *Lack of forgiveness* destroys relationships. In the same chapter where he urges Christians to "make every effort to keep the unity of the Spirit through the bond of peace," Paul emphasizes the gracious attitudes necessary for preserving unity: "Be kind and compassionate to one another, forgiving each other, just as in Christ God forgave you" (Eph 4:3, 32).

3. Intensive Care

"They shared everything they had" (Acts 4:32).

The disciples demonstrated such intense concern for one another, they even sold property if necessary to meet the needs of others in the Christian community.

For these believers, grace was no abstract concept. It meant vegetables and grain to feed a hungry family, a warm dry place to sleep, and perhaps a denarius or two for paying Caesar's taxes. Whenever a believer showed up on the doorstep of a brother or sister in need, grace took on a human face.

Even the agnostic E. R. Dodds expresses his admiration for the care-giving character of the Christian community in the early years of its history:

> Love of one's neighbor is not an exclusively Christian virtue, but in our period [second and third centuries A.D.] the Christians appear to have practiced it much more effectively than any other group. The Church provided the essentials of social security: it cared for widows and orphans, the old, the unemployed, and the disabled; it provided a burial fund for the poor and a nursing service in the time of plague. But even more important, I suspect, than these material benefits was the sense of belonging which the Christian community could give.[3]

A senior citizens minister on the staff of a large church related to me the wonderful story of a time when he was called to deal with an emergency in the home of one of the church's members. He ran to his car and rushed to the address, only to find on his arrival that the situation had already been resolved through the intervention of a care-group leader who also had heard about the need.

Graceful churches do not expect the pastoral staff to provide all the personal ministry. They find ways to involve a broad base of the congregation in intensive care-giving.

4. Aggressive Evangelism

"With great power the apostles continued to testify to the resurrection of the Lord Jesus" (Acts 4:33).

Evangelism is *an act of courage*. Men like Peter and John, who were eyewitnesses of the risen Christ, dared to proclaim the name of Jesus in the face of stiff opposition. No threats or intimidation could prevent them from speaking about what they had seen and heard (Acts 4:20). Their faith was both courageous and contagious.

Evangelism is also *an expression of friendship*. Jesus' disciples presented the gospel with honesty and respect to a wide variety of individuals: the treasurer of Ethiopia, who sought answers while sharing a chariot ride with Philip (Acts 8:26-39); a group of Greek philosophers who dialogued with Paul in the Athenian marketplace (Acts 17:17-18); and King Agrippa, who listened to Paul in the formal audience room surrounded by other high-ranking government officials (Acts 25:23-26:32).

As Donald McGavran correctly noted,

Evangelism is the friendliest possible activity. If to become a Christian, know Christ as Lord and Savior, have one's sins forgiven, and be empowered to act lovingly in this unlovely world is the pearl of great price, what greater boon can Christians confer on their neighbors than to lead them to these pearls?[4]

Evangelism is *a demonstration of patience*. Mike

came to our church two years after he received an informational brochure in the mail. Mike lives near the community center where our newly-planted church began holding worship services. Each week as he returned from his Sunday morning golf game, he noticed our church's sign on the sidewalk — but still he stayed away.

Eventually Mike found the courage to attend our worship service one Sunday. Another full year of patient teaching and friendship-building followed. Finally the day came when Mike was baptized and added to the church. If you talk to Mike now, he will laugh with you about giving up those Sunday morning golf games; but he typifies the serious-minded person who cannot be rushed into discipleship.

Even God Himself demonstrates patience as He waits for people to come to repentance (2 Pet 3:9). Patience is an indispensable ingredient in any recipe for successful outreach.

Most of all, evangelism is *an act of grace*. The apostles did not engage in evangelism to alleviate personal guilt or to achieve personal gain. They were captivated and motivated by the grace of God. Like cups filled to overflowing, the early Christians spilled over with the message of God's kindness in Christ.

5. Gracious Attitudes

"Much grace was with them all" (Acts 4:33).

I have to admit, when I read earlier descriptions of Jesus' disciples, grace is not the first word that comes to mind! They repeatedly quarreled over who was to be considered the greatest (Luke 9:46, 22:24). They became so angry and impatient with the people in a particularly resistant village, they wanted to call fire down from heaven to destroy them (Luke 9:51-55). They struggled to comprehend Jesus' kind attentiveness to people who seemed undeserving or even ungrateful (Luke 8:42-48, 17:11-19). And when he misunderstood the necessity of Jesus' sacrifice for sin, Peter even dared to rebuke the Lord and openly challenge the Master's will (Mark 8:31-33).

But God's grace changed everything. The fact of Jesus' resurrection, and the power of the Holy Spirit, transformed these men and women from brokenness to wholeness, from shallow self-centeredness to mature cooperation. They grew gracefully until, like Jesus, they became grace-givers themselves.

SUMMARY

Jesus Christ is the embodiment of grace, "full of grace and truth." To find the right balance in our own lives, we must follow Christ who not only modeled the graceful life, but transformed His followers into grace-givers as well.

Christ came to a clumsy, awkward, sin-stained world, and lived gracefully. He calls us to do the same.

NOTES: CHAPTER ONE

[1]"So here are the only two options from which a sinner may choose: (1) true Christianity, in which Christ the sin-bearer offers salvation 'by grace . . . through faith'; or (2) anything else, in which one must futilely try to save himself as a result of works. All religion, all philosophy, all of life itself comes down to this choice; and the glory of the gospel is that there is such a choice in the first place. All praise to God the Redeemer, whose infinite grace and infinite suffering have provided us ill-deserving sinners with this choice!" See Jack Cottrell, *What the Bible Says About God the Redeemer* (Joplin, MO: College Press, 1987), p. 459.

[2]J.W. McGarvey, *Acts of the Apostles*, Vol I (Cincinnati: Standard Publishing, n.d.), p. 79.

[3]E.R. Dodds, *Pagan and Christian in an Age of Anxiety* (New York: W.W. Norton & Company, 1965), pp. 136-137.

[4]Donald A. McGavran, *Momentous Decisions in Missions Today* (Grand Rapids: Baker, 1984), p. 165.

2

AN ATMOSPHERE OF GRACE

One of my favorite places is Hershey, Pennsylvania. It is a lovely town, nestled in a valley surrounded by peaceful-looking dairy farms. Everywhere you turn, you see the influence of Hershey's famous chocolate factory. Even the street lights look like candy kisses. And by mid-afternoon each day, a chocolately aroma wafts through the air, puffing out a fragrance so sweet, you almost conclude that breathing could produce tooth decay. There is something very appealing about the atmosphere in towns like Hershey.

Churches have a certain air about them too. The apostle Paul wrote that through His people, God "spreads everywhere the fragrance of the knowledge of Him" (2 Cor 2:14). Some people reject the gospel just as they would turn their noses away from a foul odor. To them, Paul says, "we are the smell of death." Those who accept God's grace in Christ, however, welcome the word of truth like a breath of fresh air. We are "the fragrance of life" to them (2 Cor 2:15-16).

It is important to ask, "What is the atmosphere in our church?" Even more, we need to consider, "What are we doing to establish an atmosphere of grace?" These questions are especially important for leaders, since our own attitudes set the tone. As someone has said, "If you want to know the temperature of your church, put the thermometer in your own mouth!"

Near the end of his life, King David described the kind of atmosphere a godly leader can create:

> When one rules over men in righteousness,
> > when he rules in the fear of God,
> He is like the light of morning at sunrise
> > on a cloudless morning,
> Like the brightness after rain
> > that brings the grass from the earth.
> > > (2 Sam 23:3b-4)

Like rain-soaked grass on a warm summer day, churches thrive in an atmosphere of grace. This is true in old rural churches like the one where I grew up in southern Ohio. As a child, I learned to sing "Jesus Loves Me" and listened to Bible stories from the lips of godly Sunday School teachers who had lived their entire lives within a mile of the church building. There was grace in that old church.

But over the years, I have also sensed an atmosphere of grace in a store-front church in New York City, in an open-air chapel in Grand Goave, Haiti, in a tiny house-church in Sanjo, Japan, and in a rented theatre where God's people gather in the heart of Caracas, Venezuela. Wherever they are located, healthy churches accept and express God's grace with clarity and enthusiasm. They know why they exist and what they are trying to do. They possess a sense of direction and destiny. They are "the church on purpose."[1]

Unhealthy churches, on the other hand, flounder in the stagnant waters of purposelessness. Without clear goals or a well-defined reason for existence, they gather weakly weekly. Without grace, they wither and die like plants deprived of sunshine and water.

Instead of the fresh, nourishing bread of life, unhealthy congregations are fed a stale diet of "shoulds." "You should be more faithful in attendance." (But *why?*) "You should be more generous in your offerings." (What is our real *motive* for giving?) "You should be more committed." (But is it also possible to find *joy* in serving the Lord?)

Many sensitive believers hunger and thirst not for more "shoulds," but for more "*coulds.*" They are asking, "How could we know God more fully? How could we love Him more deeply? How could we make a bigger difference for Christ in our neighborhood and our world? How could we be more authentic in our walk with Christ?"

Leaders spend a lot of time telling people to grow. The problem is, we seldom tell them how to grow *gracefully.*

ATMOSPHERIC CONDITIONS WHICH LEAD TO DYSGRACE AND DECLINE

Why do so many churches lack a climate for growth? Perhaps they merely mirror the graceless attitude so common in society as a whole. David Seamands observes:

> I am convinced that the basic cause of some of the most disturbing emotional/spiritual problems which trouble evangelical Christians is the failure to receive and live out God's unconditional grace, and the corresponding failure to offer that grace to others.[2]

Even in churches which teach a solid theology of grace, the message sometimes comes across merely as a propositional truth, but never gets down to what Seamands calls "gut-level grace," affecting beliefs and emotions deep in the inner person of the heart.[3]

It is possible to understand grace intellectually without really experiencing it as a daily and personal reality. Even people who have been Christians for a long time struggle with this. Many believers can *define* grace ("unmerited favor") and even *quote Scriptures* about grace ("By grace you are saved"), but their inner lives are tormented by deep feelings of inadequacy, unworthiness, and shame.

Seamands calls this *dysgrace*, a tragic distortion or impairment of grace (just as *dyspepsia* means disturbed digestion and *dyslexia* refers to an impaired ability to read).[4]

In churches afflicted by dysgrace, one can detect several unhealthy conditions which pollute the atmosphere.

Refusing People

Some churches simply shut out potential members and refuse to offer grace to anyone considered different or undesirable. It is dysgraceful when Christians refuse to reach out across barriers involving economic or social status, educational background, or skin color.

Graceful churches find ways to embrace reachable people in their ministry area, either through developing new programs or by planting new churches. In the words of C. Peter Wagner, "people blindness is a deterrent to effective evangelism."[5]

Defusing People

Another symptom of dysgrace is the tendency to stifle enthusiasm and fresh ideas.

Picture Alan, an eager new Christian whose newfound faith nearly bursts at the seams. He can hardly wait to get involved in Christian service. Alan is disappointed but not totally surprised when his unbelieving friends react negatively to his conversion. But he is bewildered and hurt when the church board reacts coolly to his proposal to start a new benevolence ministry. After a few months of encountering disinterest and roadblocks from the church bureaucracy, Alan's original zeal has turned to disillusionment.

Dysgraceful churches squelch enthusiasm, shun

creativity, and uphold the status quo at all costs. They are spiritual fire extinguishers, ready to throw cold water on the sparks of new ideas before they even have a chance to burn brightly.

"Do not put out the Spirit's fire" (1 Thess 5:19).

Confusing People

Like a farmer's crops, churches grow better in sunlight than in fog. Unfortunately, dysgraceful churches send mixed messages on important Bible issues, and thus produce more fog than light.

I once saw a cartoon which pictures a bewildered-looking group of city highway workers. Their leader pointed to a planning chart and said, "To avoid confusion, we decided to rearrange the streets alphabetically: Fifth Street, First Street, Fourth Street, Second Street, Sixth Street, Third Street."

Unnecessary complexity leads to perplexity. Paul warned Timothy to watch out for those who confuse and sidetrack the church (see Appendix One, page 209). Quarreling about words, he said, "is of no value, and only ruins those who listen" (2 Tim 2:14).

To grow gracefully, a church has to do more than quarrel over words. Healthy churches uphold Biblical essentials (Eph 4:1-6) while allowing personal liberty in matters of opinion (Rom 14:1-15:6). There must be a clear and unmistakable commitment to Christ and His Word, and a clearly articulated philosophy of ministry for accomplishing Christ's purpose through the local church.

"God is not a God of disorder but of peace" (1 Cor 14:33).

Amusing People

Genuine joy abounds in graceful churches, just as it does in healthy families. There is something holy and healing in the hearty laughter of Christians who have learned to "rejoice with those who rejoice" just as they "mourn with those who mourn" (Rom 12:15). God's grace enables us to "rejoice in the Lord always" (Phil 4:4).

Dysgraceful churches seldom experience real joy. Instead, they offer shallow entertainment and "gospel gimmicks" intended to draw and amuse a crowd. Nowhere is this symptom more prevalent than in the consumer-oriented United States. As someone has said, "To the early church, Christianity was a faith; the Greeks made it a philosophy; and the Americans have made it an enterprise."[6]

No one seriously disputes the value of interesting preaching, quality music, attractive facilities, and appealing programs. But evangelism can never be reduced to putting on a good show. Discipleship is more than mere feel-good-ism.

Church programs must be closely linked to the graceful purpose of Christ, or they can actually become a distraction and a deterrent to authentic spiritual growth.

Amusing people is not enough. "Even in laughter the heart may ache, and joy may end in grief" (Proverbs 14:13).

Abusing People

In extreme cases, dysgrace may best be described as outright spiritual abuse.

David Johnson and Jeff Van Vonderen have identified the following dynamics which are at work in spiritually abusive systems:

1. *Power-posturing.* Leaders demand excessive amounts of authority and compel their followers to submit.

2. *Performance preoccupation.* Spirituality is mea-

sured by strict adherence to the church's rules with little emphasis on grace.

3. *Unspoken rules*. According to the "can't talk" rule, for example, any expression of disagreement or dissent is viewed as disloyalty toward the church's leadership.

4. *Lack of balance*. Abusive churches may either overemphasize subjective experiences, or go to the other extreme and allow no room for the personal leading of God's Spirit.

5. *Paranoia*. Such churches are dominated by suspicion and fear of outsiders, and discourage interaction with the outside world.

6. *Misplaced loyalty*. Loyalty to Christ becomes identified exclusively with one's involvement in a particular congregation or organization.

7. *Secretiveness*. Rather than dealing with important issues and problems with an appropriate degree of openness, abusive systems consistently handle such matters behind closed doors.[7]

In his book, *Churches That Abuse*, Ronald Enroth contends that abusive churches misuse spiritual authority; control people through fear, guilt, and threats; foster rigidity; discourage questions; and make leaving painful. According to Enroth, "All that is needed for abuse is a pastor accountable to no one and therefore beyond confrontation," a leader who says in effect, "It's my way or the highway."[8]

These, then, are the atmospheric conditions which lead to dysgrace and decline: *refusing* people, *defusing* people, *confusing* people, *amusing* people, and *abusing* people. The common thread is that dysgraceful churches are **using people** instead of ministering to them.

Graceful churches recognize the incalculable value of every person for whom Christ died. But in dysgraceful churches, people are merely numbers to be counted, supporters to be manipulated, or crowds to be entertained.

What, then, are the *right* atmospheric conditions for growing gracefully? How can we escape from the smog of dysgrace?

ATMOSPHERIC CONDITIONS WHICH LEAD TO GRACE AND GROWTH

The Congregational Self-Image Factor

Just like individual persons, churches have a self-image which may be either positive or negative.

Graceless churches usually have a negative view of themselves: an ecclesiastical inferiority complex. We could call them "L.O.S.E. churches," for being part of such a congregation "Lowers Our Self Esteem." L.O.S.E. churches experience loss of morale, loss of spiritual power, and eventually loss of members. Often, the buildings and grounds of such churches fall into disrepair and neglect, outward symptoms of a deeper problem. The meetings in L.O.S.E. churches are dominated by negative attitudes and debates over trivialities. L.O.S.E. churches *fixate* on problems, but seldom actually *fix* problems. The prevailing attitude is reactive rather than proactive, negative instead of positive, obstacle-focused instead of opportunity-focused. Seldom do the members of a L.O.S.E. church hear a sermon about God's grace.

While many factors contribute to this problem, the major cause may be graceless, visionless leadership. Just as parents profoundly impact their child's self-image, church leaders shape the church's view of itself. Arguably, one of the most important functions of a church leader is to build up the members' image of themselves as the grace-filled people of God, thus establishing an atmosphere for growth.

Graceful churches could be called "W.I.N." churches, for they live by the grace-full philosophy, "We're Improving Now!" They know they have not arrived at their final destination yet. They do not claim to have some magic formula. But in W.I.N. churches, people are open to do what it takes to grow. They are willing to try, eager to make progress.

W.I.N. churches feel good about themselves, not because of their own accomplishments, but because they have learned to accept and abide in the grace of God. Their leaders have helped them discover the life-changing reality of 1 Peter 2:9-10:

> But you are a chosen people, a royal priesthood, a holy nation, a people belonging to God, that you may declare the praises of Him who called you out of darkness into His wonderful light.
> Once you were not a people, but now you are the people of God; once you had not received mercy, but now you have received mercy.

Members of W.I.N. churches speak enthusiastically about their church, its program, and its leaders. Because they find security in Christ, W.I.N. churches are free to reach out. They find it completely natural to share their excitement with friends and neighbors. Visitors find a genuine welcome.

The Faithfulness Factor

Another characteristic of a healthy growth atmosphere is *faithfulness*. Unfortunately, however, even the term "faithful" is sometimes used to justify stagnation. Some defend the status quo by saying, "No, we're not growing. But at least we're being faithful!"

What, then, is faithfulness?

Faithfulness means relationships. Nowhere is this truth better demonstrated than in Ruth's famous

41

promise to her mother-in-law Naomi (Ruth 1:16-17). If we are faithful people, we will be: (1) Loyal to our immediate family ("Where you go I will go"); (2) Loyal to our spiritual family ("Your people will be my people"); (3) Loyal to the Lord ("Your God will be my God"), and (4) Loyal until death ("Where you die, I will die"). Faithfulness is lived out in lasting, deepening, grace-filled personal relationships.

Faithfulness means success. Jesus promised the church in Smyrna, "Be faithful, even to the point of death, and I will give you the crown of life" (Rev 2:10). Healthy churches do not measure success by comparison with other churches, but by steadfast service to Christ.

Nevertheless, *faithfulness means productivity.* Healthy churches do not shrink from the task of doing all they can for the glory of their gracious Savior.

In Jesus' parable of the talents (Matt 25:14-30), the five-talent man and the two-talent man were called "good and faithful servants" because they used their master's resources to produce a result commensurate with their potential. As Joe Ellis notes, "In simplest terms, Jesus defines faithfulness (or success) as accomplishing as much as possible with the resources one has." Unfaithfulness, by contrast, means "failure to produce what we can."[9]

The third servant in Jesus' parable — the man who received only one talent — hid his master's money in the ground. Ellis comments:

> That third servant is intriguing. He is not a scoundrel or a thief. He didn't steal the money. He didn't misappropriate it. He didn't waste it. He didn't risk it. He didn't lose it. He preserved it intact! At first glance we might consider him a good man. He kept with scrupulous care what was entrusted to him. He buried it where it would be safe and guarded it.

> . . . But the master calls him in various translations, wicked, lazy, slothful, unprofitable, worthless, useless, unproductive, *unfaithful*. How shattering! Is there anything worse to call him?
>
> According to Jesus' standard, to fail we don't have to run amuck and do something dreadful. We don't have to deny the faith. We don't have to adopt some doctrinal heresy. . . . To fail as the Master's servants we don't have to do any of these things. To fail, all we have to do is *nothing!*[10]

Faithfulness means risk-taking. As George Hunter has noted, the church needs to be "a community that both cares and dares."[11] Graceful churches dare to chase what George Barna calls "the most possible dream."[12] They are excited about the future, passionate about the possibilities awaiting them.

The Encouragement Factor

A couple of years ago, a crowd gathered by the Ohio River to watch as a demolition crew blew up a part of an old bridge. After waiting for hours, the sizeable crowd heard a quick explosion, and in moments, a big section of the bridge collapsed into the muddy water to the cheers of the watching throng.

It is fascinating to ponder the fact that so many people will show up to watch the moment when a bridge comes down, but very few stand watching during the many months it takes to build a bridge.

In a world preoccupied with destruction, Christians are God's construction crew. Our job is to patiently offer grace to the disgraceful, hope to the hopeless, and faith to the frustrated.

To live and work in today's world is to encounter an environment where often is heard a discouraging word. Lacking the life-giving nourishment of God's grace, people suffer from an "emotional vitamin A deficiency":

Acceptance, Affection, and Affirmation.[13]

Christians can make a difference, but only if our churches offer a consistent atmosphere of encouragement.

The Prayer Factor

The most important ingredient of a growth atmosphere is *prayer*.

Speaking of the temple in Jerusalem, Jesus said, "My house will be called a house of prayer" (Matt 21:13). Today Jesus' "house" is in the hearts of His people, not in a temple of stone. But His church must still be a house of prayer.

In the book of Acts, God's people were *devoted* to prayer (Acts 2:42). They surrounded *decisions* with prayer (Acts 1:23-26, 6:3-6). The found *comfort* and developed *courage* through prayer (Acts 4:23-31).

Growing gracefully means relying completely on God. Prayer serves as a declaration of dependence — an admission that growth comes not by man's might or power, but by the Spirit of God (Zech 4:6).

SUMMARY

Churches thrive in an atmosphere of grace. Instead of using people, healthy churches infuse people with the exciting realization of their potential in Christ.

Breathing the life-giving oxygen of grace, a church can begin to fulfill the Psalmist's vision of godly growth, and become "like a tree planted by streams of water, which yields its fruit in season" (Ps 1:3).

NOTES: CHAPTER TWO

[1]Joe S. Ellis, *The Church on Purpose* (Cincinnati: Standard Publishing, 1982), p. 33.

[2]David A. Seamands, *Healing Grace* (Wheaton, IL: Victor Books, 1988), p. 14.

[3]*Ibid.*, p. 27.

[4]*Ibid.*, p. 45.

[5]C. Peter Wagner, *Your Church Can Grow* (Ventura, CA: Regal Books, 1976), p. 134.

[6]John Dawson, *Taking Our Cities for God* (Lake Mary, FL: Creation House, 1989), p. 193.

[7]David Johnson and Jeff Van Vonderen, *The Subtle Power of Spiritual Abuse* (Minneapolis: Bethany House, 1991), pp. 63-79.

[8]Ronald Enroth, *Churches That Abuse* (Grand Rapids: Zondervan, 1992), pp. 189, 196.

[9]Joe S. Ellis, *The Church on Target* (Cincinnati: Standard Publishing, 1986), pp. 37-38.

[10]*Ibid.*, p. 38.

[11]George G. Hunter, *The Contagious Congregation* (Nashville: Abingdon, 1979), p. 142.

[12]George Barna, *The Power of Vision* (Ventura, CA: Regal Books, 1992), p. 30.

[13]Seamands, *Healing Grace*, p. 49.

3

KEEPING CHURCH SIMPLE

You may never have heard the name of Gutzon Borglum, but you know about his work. Borglum's greatest sculpture was finished in 1941. It required fourteen years, 360 stonecutters, and removal of 450,000 tons of rock.[1]

Borglum's work of art is on display year-round in South Dakota. Towering from the granite peaks of Mt. Rushmore, the carefully-carved faces of four American presidents bear quiet testimony to the skill of their designer.

Yet the artistry of Almighty God far surpasses any human creation. Our Maker formed this complex universe with such divine intricacy that you can see His designer label on the stars of the sky, the trees of the forest, the beasts of the field, and the fish of the sea. And God stamped a special designer label on men and women who are made in His image.

THE COMPLICATED CONGREGATION

A Complex Body

Our physical bodies are amazingly complicated, yet designed for efficient operation. The human heart pumps seventy-five gallons of blood per hour through a 60,000-mile vascular network.

The brain contains twelve billion neurons organized with incredible intricacy. Six hundred million tiny thin-walled sacs in the lungs called alveoli make it possible for our bodies to receive much needed oxygen.[2]

Likewise, the spiritual body of Christ is fearfully and wonderfully made. The church displays the order, complexity, and grandeur of her Creator. We are God's workmanship (Eph 2:10) and God's household (Eph 2:19). We share in God's promises (Eph 3:6). Through us He demonstrates His wisdom, power, and glory (Eph 3:10, 20,21).

In 1 Corinthians 12, Paul uses the analogy of the human body to show God's orderly arrangement of His people:

> *Every person is a part* — "Now you are the body of Christ, and each one of you is a part of it" (v. 27).
> *Every person has a partner* — "If one part suffers, every part suffers with it; if one part is honored, every part rejoices with it" (v. 26).
> *Every part has a purpose* — "But in fact God has arranged the parts in the body, every one of them, just as He wanted them to be" (v. 18).

A Blessed Blend

Churches are remarkably complicated. No other group or association on earth contains such a wide variety of people.[3] Christians are wonderfully mixed-up people — not confused, but combined in a delightful mixture where Jews and Greeks, slaves and free, males and females find oneness in Christ (Gal 3:28). Where else but in the church can you find such a blessed blend?

The *ethnic-mix* joins together people from different nations and cultures. I enjoyed the ethnic diversity of the congregation I served in New York. When our church choir stood up to sing, the lyrics rang out in accents ranging from German to Spanish, from Tagalog (Filipino) to Brooklynese. We "made a joyful noise" as our accents blended together in heartfelt praise. At our fellowship dinners, the table might contain a platter of Puerto Rican rice and beans next to a Filipino dish called *pan sit*, served with Italian baked ziti and Irish soda bread!

The *age-mix* enables both young and old to interact in the church. Since my children were very small, every Sunday they have rubbed elbows with wise old saints, fun-loving teens, hard-working middle-aged adults, and other children their own age. Where? In the church!

No one can measure, but no one can deny, the wholesome impact of the young woman who teaches the Beginner class each week, or the long-married couple who take two newlyweds under their wing, or the senior citizen who faithfully prays for the youth of her church. Older men and women provide indispensable role models for the young (Titus 2:2-8). And the young can offer priceless encouragement and honor for the old (1 Tim 4:12, 5:1-2).

The *maturity-mix* blends new believers with others who have longer experience in the faith. For example, my congregation includes two middle-aged men named Mark. Mark Number One has been a Christian for many years; Mark Number Two became a believer just a couple of years ago. In their own unique ways, both of these men are "making their mark" in our church and community — and we need them both!

Babes in Christ infuse the church with enthusiasm, fresh ideas, and insightful questions — and they provide direct pipelines for taking the gospel to their unsaved family and friends. Mature Christians provide needed stability, seasoned counsel, and models of godly living (Phil 3:17).

Perhaps most remarkable is the *gift-mix* found in the body of Christ. "We have different gifts, according to the grace given to us" (Rom 12:6). Even a small congregation demonstrates the blessed blend of believers who use their God-given abilities in areas like teaching, encouraging, and extending mercy. God manages to blend together the speaker and the server (1 Pet 4:10-11), the sufferer and the honoree (1 Cor 12:26), the leader and the follower (Heb 13:7, 17), the married and the single (1 Cor 7:32-40), the rich and the poor (Acts 4:32-35), the strong and the weak (Gal 6:1-2). Only the Holy Spirit could turn such a complicated hodgepodge of people into a harmonious body that works together for the common good.

A Needed Balance

Church growth is seldom easy. It is often complicated. Joe Ellis has rightly observed that "the key to a successful church does not involve one single aspect of church life, but a complex balance of several: doctrinal, functional, and empirical matters, plus a solid dependence upon God through faith."[4]

Plans, programs, people and problems demand attention and can almost seem overwhelming. Further, churches pass through different seasons of life. There are times to come together for fellowship and times to reach out for evangelism. There are times to *rest* in prayer, and times to *wrestle* in prayer. There are times to weep and times to laugh, times to be silent and times to speak up (Eccl 3:1-8). There are times to begin something new, and times to restore something old. Some ministers are called to lay a foundation, others to continue building upon the foundation (1 Cor 3:9-11). As Max Lucado has said, "Ministry is done in chapters, and wise is the minister who knows his page number."[5]

Clearly, churches are complicated — but they do not have to be *overcomplicated*. It is man, not our graceful God, who authors confusion and weighs down the body of Christ with outmoded traditions, unnecessary programs, and unhelpful busyness. It is man, not God, who allows different ethnic backgrounds, different ages, different levels of maturity, different opinions or different gifts to divide or detour the church. Our God of grace "is not a God of disorder but of peace" (1 Cor 14:33).

When I hear of churches battling over bylaws or quarreling over carpet colors, I remember reading about a major league pitcher who frustrated his manager and fans because he overanalyzed every pitch and worried over every movement of his body as he threw the ball.

"His problem is that he spends too much time fretting over things that really don't matter," one of his teammates complained. "He'll be a great pitcher if he will just learn to stand on the mound and throw the ball. Pitching is simpler than he thinks!"

Unfortunately, churches make the same mistake when we become preoccupied with the complexities of our own body life and forget our primary purpose: giving glory to our gracious God.

Our Lord, the master designer, can handle any problem our churches face. His presence is near. His instructions are clear. His grace is abundant. We need to trust God with the complications and get on with His work.

THE SIMPLIFIED CONGREGATION

A few years ago, a copy machine manufacturer advertised its product with the slogan, "We just make great copiers." Unlike our competitors, the ads insisted, we do not try to make typewriters, tape recorders, and microwave ovens. We do one thing, and we do it well.

Such a single-minded approach communicates well

in today's world where specialization is so common. Physicians specialize in certain areas of medicine. Mechanics specialize in particular types of cars or trucks. The best cheesecake I ever ate came from a bakery which makes nothing but cheesecake! I know a carpenter who identifies his special area of expertise by calling his business "Just Decks."

Of course, these skillful workers could do other things. But in each of these examples, the workers recognize that they will be more effective if they are single-minded and focused.

Perhaps our congregations could learn something from these examples. Healthy churches are unafraid to ask themselves the hard questions: "Out of all the good things we could do, are we actually doing the most important things? Are we singleminded and focused? Do we understand our purpose? How well are we accomplishing it?"

The apostle Paul wore many hats. Besides serving as an apostle, preacher, and teacher, Paul also was a world traveler, a prolific writer, a "troubleshooter" for problem churches, a "consultant" who advised young ministers, a fund-raiser, and sometimes a professional tentmaker! Yet despite his many responsibilities and concerns, Paul sounds surprisingly single-minded when he says, *"One thing I do:* Forgetting what is behind and straining toward what is ahead, I press on toward the goal to win the prize for which God has called me heavenward in Christ Jesus" (Phil 3:13-14, italics mine).

Have we forgotten this secret? Unfortunately, churches can become so overcomplicated and cumbersome that they make little progress toward the goal. A race horse will not win the Kentucky Derby if it is carrying 300 pounds of baggage on its back. A driver will not win the Indianapolis 500 if he leaves the track for an hour to tour the city of Indianapolis!

When there is a race to win, sensible racers put aside unnecessary baggage and avoid unnecessary diversions. We will never accomplish Christ's purpose if our churches are loaded down with committees that are not committed, bored boards, "services" that do not lead to greater service, or lots of programs but little prayer.

Some churches have exchanged the freedom of simplicity for a flurry of activity. A maze of confusion has replaced amazing grace.

Many of us need to simplify our congregations. At its root, the word "simple" means single or undivided. Simple does not have to mean shallow, slipshod, or overly simplistic. Nor does a "simple congregation" have to mean a "small congregation." In fact, large churches are often more successful than others in focusing on their task of disciple-making (which is one reason they have grown large in the first place).

In simplified congregations, the leaders: (1) keep clear Christ-centered goals before the people, (2) insist that all programs of the church contribute in some way to the accomplishment of these goals, and (3) communicate these goals clearly. Here are some other characteristics of these simplified congregations.

Uncomplicated Preaching and Teaching

Jesus was a master at couching spiritual depth in clear, direct words. His Sermon on the Mount began with the incomparable Beatitudes and ended with the simple but powerful story of the wise and foolish builders. In between, Jesus provided straightforward insight on such practical matters as anger, sexual morality, divorce, prayer, money, worry, and dealing with one's enemies.

In His sermon in John 6, Jesus used a familiar food

to illustrate some hard teachings about His own identity and His saving work: "I am the bread of life," He said. Jesus did not come to impress people with His well-crafted outlines and rhetorical style; He came to seek and to save the lost. When men rejected Him, it was not because he left them confused but because they were unwilling to accept His clear claims and His call to discipleship.

Admittedly, when Paul wrote letters to strengthen the faith of Christians, his teachings were often challenging and at times "hard to understand" (2 Pet 3:16). But Paul's normal preaching style was direct and unmistakable. He made people uncomfortable because he spoke so clearly about pointed issues like faith in Christ, righteousness, self-control and the judgment to come (as in Acts 24:24,25).

Peter wrote eloquently about great themes like the new birth, holiness, and the significance of Jesus' death and resurrection (1 Peter chapters 1-3). But he also knew how to apply these truths to the hearts and lives of his listeners so they would be moved to action (Acts 2:36-41).

In the simplified congregation, preachers and teachers truly communicate the Word. The sermons are not just theological theorizing, and the lessons are not just aimless discussion. Bible truths are explained and applied.

Uncomplicated Personal Evangelism

Countless books have been written about evangelism, but no one has ever improved on the simple approach Andrew used when he found his brother Simon Peter and told him, "We have found the Messiah" (John 1:41). In the simplified congregation, evangelism occurs as people reach out through their natural networks of family members, friends, neighbors, and coworkers.

Personal referral is a simple but powerful technique. When my house needed to be covered with vinyl siding, I wanted to find a reliable contractor to do the work. The company I eventually hired got the job because of the enthusiastic recommendation of two trusted friends. Likewise, as we develop relationships of trust and friendship with others, we will find opportunities to recommend our Lord and His saving grace. We will be able to give answers to everyone who asks the reason for our hope (1 Pet 3:15).

In the simplified congregation, each member takes seriously the attitude expressed in Paul's three "I am's" in Romans 1:14-16: (1) *"I am obligated"* (under orders from the Lord to share His good news); (2) *"I am eager"* (to proclaim the Word is a joy and a privilege); (3) *"I am not ashamed"* (for the gospel is the power of God unto salvation).

Uncomplicated Approach to Ministry

Simplified congregations are busy serving, not compelling their people to attend countless meetings that start at 7:00 sharp and end at 10:00 dull. Time is seldom wasted.[6] Members focus their efforts on areas where they are gifted and highly motivated. Leaders lead and followers follow; there is a high level of interpersonal trust. Organizational structure is simple and efficient: functioning as a body, not a bureaucracy, the church can meet needs quickly without going through several layers of red tape.

Common sense prevails. Facilities are kept clean, functional, and appealing. Newcomers can easily find their way to the visitor welcome center, the nursery, and the restroom. Problems are addressed as quickly and decisively as possible. Just as the highway department will quickly remove a stalled car that could block traffic for miles, the church must deal with unresolved conflict that could block the forward movement of the entire congregation.

In the simplified congregation, prayer is not a program but a priority. "Do this in remembrance of me" is not just a ritual but a reality. Fellowship is not just a feeling but a fact. These are simple concepts, but like sheep we easily stray from them down winding pathways that lead us farther from our Shepherd.[7]

SUMMARY

Henry Thoreau once said: "Our life is frittered away by detail. Simplify. Simplify."

While driving across Missouri, I noticed a farm near the highway where someone had built a long fence out of nothing but old wagon wheels fastened together side by side. I had to admit, this one-of-a-kind fence was eye catching. It must have required considerable effort and expense to locate, purchase, and bind together all those wheels. Yet there was something unnatural about a row of carefully-arranged wheels just sitting there not moving. Wheels are made to roll, to move, to go places — not just to serve as a decoration or a barrier to keep out intruders.

It is simple, really. Our churches do not need to reinvent the wheel. We just need to keep moving with the one we have.

NOTES: CHAPTER THREE

[1]"Mt. Rushmore Gets Long-Delayed Dedication," *Cincinnati Enquirer*, July 4, 1991.

[2]Charles R. Schroeder, *The Human Body: Its Structure and Function*, (Dubuque, IA: Wm. C. Brown Co., 1971), pp. 15-24, 38.

[3]It is true that most congregations tend to attract people from a similar ethnic or socioeconomic background. People tend to be drawn to congregations where they can identify with the language, music, dress, and other lifestyle traits of the people. But we need to be careful not to overstate the case for sameness in the church. Even in the very small congregations, there is a great diversity as Christ binds together His people (see Colossians 3:11).

[4]Joe S. Ellis, *The Church on Target*, (Cincinnati: Standard Publishing, 1986), p. 78.

[5]Max Lucado, "The Applause of Heaven and Earth," *Leadership*, Summer, 1992, p. 17.

[6]Researcher George Barna argues that as time becomes increasingly precious, people will be more reluctant to get involved in any volunteer activity they perceive as poorly planned or a waste of time. See George Barna, *The Frog in the Kettle* (Ventura, CA: Regal, 1990), pp. 39-47.

[7]An old Shaker hymn reminds us: "It's a gift to be simple, It's a gift to be free, It's a gift to come down where you ought to be." Quoted by Richard J. Foster in *Celebration of Discipline* (San Francisco: Harper & Row, 1978), p. 69.

4

HELPERS IN THE HARVEST:
REACHING OUT GRACEFULLY

I grew up on a farm in southern Ohio. You learn many lessons on a farm, but perhaps the most important lesson I learned was simply this: WHEN THE HARVEST IS READY, YOU HELP!

Every member of our family understood that helping with the harvest was not optional. The question was not, "Will I help with the harvest?" It was simply, "*How* will I help with the harvest?"

Even as a little boy, I worked alongside my older brothers stacking bales of hay on a wagon as it bumped and lurched across the field behind Dad's old tractor. It was hot, dirty work. There were different chores to be done, but every member of the family helped somehow.

After all, to be successful in farming, you have to do more than just maintain the farm in good condition; you have to harvest the crop. The job was too big for any one person to do it alone; the opportunities provided by good weather left no room for delay. My dad often reminded us, "You have to make hay while the sun shines" — his way of explaining the urgent necessity of bringing in the harvest.

After we finally stuffed the last bale of hay into the barn, we headed to the house for a cool shower and a tasty Mom-cooked meal of homemade bread, fresh roast beef, and vegetables from our garden. Helping in the harvest brought its own special rewards. Our muscles ached, and our hands and arms bore scratches from the hay-stubble; but as we sipped glasses of iced tea on a cool summer evening, every member of the family felt a sense of satisfaction. WHEN THE HARVEST IS READY, YOU HELP.

Graceful churches put this simple truth into practice. As Jesus urged, they open their eyes and look at the fields which are ripe for harvest (John 4:35). But they do more than just look; they get involved. They recognize the urgency of the task, and understand that churches exist to bring in the harvest, not just to "maintain the farm." The harvest is too big for one person to do all the work. It requires the combined effort of every member of God's family.

In graceful churches, reaching out is not considered an optional sidelight for some but a priority for all. There are different roles and tasks to be fulfilled, but everyone finds a way to participate — because WHEN THE HARVEST IS READY, YOU HELP.

WHY HELP WITH THE HARVEST?

Matthew 9:35-38 reveals three motivations for helping in God's harvest field.

1. The Harvest is Possible

"Jesus went through all the towns and villages, teaching in their synagogues, preaching the good news of the kingdom and healing every disease and sickness" (Matt 9:35).

It is tempting nowadays to see the problems instead of the potential of our neighborhoods. Especially in the great cities of our world, many tend to think only of the "three C's": Crowds, Crime, and Corruption. Jesus, however, recognized the possibilities of the towns and villages, not just the problems there. He brought instruction, healing, and grace.

On the surface, Jesus' mission seemed improbable at best. There were no televisions or radios to broadcast His message, no cars or planes to expedite travel. His Jewish nation wielded little political power. Some of the towns and villages He visited resisted His message. In Nazareth, Jesus' hometown, the people who heard His Bible lesson in the synagogue tried to throw Jesus over a cliff (Luke 4:16-30). The people in one Samaritan village were so hard-hearted and stubborn, James and John wanted to call down fire from heaven and destroy it (Luke 9:51-55). Members of Jesus' own family did not believe in Him at first (John 7:3-5), and at one point even tried to take charge of Him, thinking He was out of His mind (Mark 3:20-21). Jesus seemed engaged in a mission impossible.

Yet Jesus lived by the principle, "All things are possible with God" (Mark 10:27). Like a microscopic mustard seed which grows into a large tree, Jesus' tiny band of followers eventually grew into a crowd that had to be counted in the thousands (Acts 2:41, 4:4).

The harvest is indeed possible. To grow gracefully, we need renewed confidence in the possibilities of faith. Galatians 6:9 assures us, "at the proper time we will reap a harvest if we do not give up." As an old Chinese proverb says, "Man who say it cannot be done should not disturb man doing it!"

2. The Harvest is Personal

Jesus saw more than crowds of people; He saw the *needs* of people. He gazed upon them with a discerning look of grace. "When He saw the crowds, He had compassion on them, because they were harassed and helpless, like sheep without a shepherd" (Matt 9:36).

The people were *harassed*. Actually, the word (from the Greek *skullo*) means to be weary, distressed, troubled, or annoyed. The same term is used in Mark 5:35 and Luke 8:49 when men reported that Jairus' daughter was dead, so there was no need to "bother" or "trouble" the Master anymore. Jesus, however, assured Jairus with the words, "Don't be afraid; just believe" (Mark 5:36). Another time, a centurion used this term when he sent word to Jesus, "Don't *trouble* yourself, for I do not deserve to have you come under my roof" (Luke 7:6, italics mine). Even when others did not want to bother Jesus, He was concerned about the things that bothered or troubled them.

The people were *helpless*. This word (from the Greek *ripto*) meant to be thrown or cast down, and thus is sometimes translated "downcast." It describes someone who falls down onto the ground in great weakness, like a person who is dying from starvation or thirst and has no strength to go on.

The people were *like sheep without a shepherd*. Sheep are vulnerable animals. They need to be led, they need to be fed, and they need to be protected. Jesus, the Good Shepherd, saw the real condition of the restless and directionless multitudes.

Jesus *had compassion* on them. The word translated "compassion" (Greek *splagchnizomai*) expresses a deep feeling of tenderness or concern. It is the word used to describe the way Jesus' "heart went out" to the widow in Nain whose only son had died (Luke 7:13), and it portrays the father's emotion as he hugs and kisses his prodigal son who returned home (Luke 15:20). The same word describes Jesus' concern for the leper who came seeking healing (Mark 1:41), and for the crowd which had run out of food after three days of instruction (Mark 8:2). Jesus' heart was moved by compassion when He saw the needs of people He loved.

The Bible mentions three times Jesus cried, and each time was related to the hurts of others. He cried at the grave of His friend Lazarus (John 11:35); He cried over the unrepentant city of Jerusalem (Luke 19:41); and He cried in the Garden of Gethsemane — not with selfish tears for His own griefs, but with the heartfelt agony of a sinless sacrifice who must bear the sins of the world (Matt 26:37-38, Heb 4:7). The Lord expressed grace emotionally as well as conceptually.

Several years ago, my wife and I attended a missionary conference in Mexico. One afternoon our missionary friends took us into the mountains to a little village of tiny adobe huts where the people still cook their meals on mud stoves. As we visited with some of the adults in the village, children began to flock around us, eager to see their American visitors. We quickly reached into our pockets and gave them little pieces of hard candy we had brought along. They smiled and said, "Gracias!" My heart ached with compassion as the children gratefully received our little gifts which seemed so short-lived and feeble in comparison with their great need. When we drove away from the village that afternoon, I thanked God for the missionaries there who consistently provide more than candy to the children of that village. They bring the life-saving bread of life.

Why help with the harvest? Because the harvest is personal — priceless people made in the image of God.

When churches grow gracefully, precious lost sheep are brought back into God's flock. During my ministry in New York, I saw the Good Shepherd's grace transform John, a former member of a street gang in Brooklyn, into a caring husband and father who developed an effective outreach ministry to Jehovah's Witnesses in the New York area. God's grace rescued Frank, our local mailman who used to try to deliver mail while experiencing alcoholic blackouts. Frank and his wife became Christians, and though he still delivers the mail, now he occasionally delivers a message for

Jesus too!

Every time the church gathers for worship, I marvel at the people God's harvest has gathered in: a tall black fellow who formerly played professional football sharing a hymnal with a little retarded girl with long blonde hair, a confused teenage boy from a dysfunctional family who has grown into a mature and dedicated Christian leader, an older couple who have found peace in their twilight years through knowing Christ.

3. The Harvest Is Plentiful

Jesus said, "The harvest is plentiful but the workers are few" (Matt 9:37).

The two enormous skyscrapers of the World Trade Center tower over lower Manhattan in New York City. When my family visited there a few years ago, we stood in a crowded elevator with dozens of tourists from all around the world whose foreign accents buzzed around us. Soon we arrived on the observation deck, and from our roof-top vantage point, we looked down upon New York's crowded streets where millions live and work. I wondered how the Lord must feel as He views all the people of the earth from His heavenly vantage point. Standing there 110 stories above the ground, a tear came to my eye as I pondered the sad irony of the World Trade Center brochure which I held in my hand. Its headline read, "The World Trade Center: This is the Closest to Heaven Many of Us Will Ever Get."

The harvest is plentiful. The church cannot just stand watching from an ivory tower while countless people drift farther from heaven every day. God calls us to be graceful people who view the crowded cities of our world as harvest fields filled with potential disciples of Jesus Christ. In Jonah's day, even the wicked city of Nineveh was the object of God's compassion, for it contained "more than a hundred and twenty thousand people who cannot tell their right hand from their left, and many cattle as well." The Lord's haunting question to Jonah still motivates all of us who want to be helpers in God's harvest: "Should I not be concerned about that great city?" (Jonah 4:11).

Though the world's needs seem overwhelming, we are not powerless to help. In fact, Jesus gave specific instructions about the course of action we should take since the harvest is so large: "Ask the Lord of the harvest, therefore, to send out workers into His harvest field" (Matt 9:38).

I will never forget the evening when I led a group of new Christians in a study of Matthew 9:35-38. After I explained that Jesus wanted us to pray for workers to serve in God's harvest field, I noticed one lady in the group raise her hand. She was a German woman named Waltraut (we all called her "Wally"), who had only been a Christian for a few months. She asked me, "David, do we do this?" I said, "What do you mean, Wally?" She continued, "You said Jesus wants us to pray for workers to go into God's harvest field, but I have been attending this church for quite some time now and I have never heard us actually do this."

Wally's words surprised and humbled me. She was right — we had not been praying for workers as Jesus asked us to do. As the group continued our discussion, we decided to spend the rest of that evening's Bible study in prayer that God would indeed raise up workers for His harvest field, including members of our own congregation and our own families.

God sometimes says "no" when we pray. But one prayer God wants to answer with a "yes" is the prayer for harvest-workers.

It is interesting that in the last verse of Matthew chapter 9, Jesus urged His disciples to pray for workers to be sent. Then in the next few verses (Matt 10:1-5), He called twelve of the disciples and sent them out. Apparently, if we pray for workers to go, we must also be willing to be sent!

Since we are surrounded by a vast ocean of human need, we should not be surprised when we feel we are "in over our heads." Truly, the harvest is too big to accomplish in our own strength — which is precisely the reason we must grow *gracefully!* Our heavenly Father blesses people who pray, "Lord of the harvest, send me out! Put me to work in your harvest field. The needs are great, and I am only one helper — but I am willing to be used. Cast me out into the depths of your missionary task where I might sink on my own but will swim by the power of God!"

Graceful churches are filled with people who want to help with God's work, not merely out of obligation, but because they are challenged by the possibilities of the harvest, moved with compassion by the personal nature of the harvest, and convinced that the harvest is indeed plentiful.

In graceful churches, people understand: WHEN THE HARVEST IS READY, YOU HELP!

PRINCIPLES OF GRACEFUL HARVESTING

You cannot rush a harvest. Successful evangelism usually results from patience, not impatience; from gentle cultivation, not forceful manipulation. Scripture uses an agricultural illustration to show the importance of patience while we wait for Jesus' return: "See how the farm waits for the land to yield its valuable crop and how patient he is for the fall and spring rains" (Jas 5:7).

Jesus used a similar example in His "parable of the growing seed":

He also said, 'This is what the kingdom of God is like. A man scatters seed on the ground. Night and day, whether he sleeps or gets up, the seed sprouts and grows, *though he does not know how*. All by itself the soil produces grain — first the stalk, then the head, then the full kernel in the head. As soon as the grain is ripe, he puts the sickle to it, because the harvest has come' (Mark 4:26-20, italics mine).

Even with the vast amount of knowledge we possess today about agriculture and horticulture, the farmer *does not know how growth occurs*. Wise farmers cooperate with God's grace expressed through natural laws, but no one can fully explain growth or force growth to happen. Jesus' parable underscores the necessity of God's grace in church growth.

The farmer plants the seed, and in some cases he irrigates and cultivates, but he does not make it grow. He does not even know how it grows. Even after all the scientific progress of recent years, the process of growth is still mysterious in many ways. So it is in the kingdom of God. Men plant the seed of the gospel, but God gives the increase. See 1 Corinthians 3:6,7.

. . . The farmer does not understand the process of growth, but he sows the seed and reaps the harvest. So it is with the worker in God's kingdom. He does not understand all about how men are redeemed, how they grow in grace, how the kingdom develops, but he does work his Lord assigns and he reaps eternal reward.[1]

Church growth cannot be reduced to a simple step-by-step formula. Graceful harvesters recognize that the sovereignty and providence of God supersede even the most clever humanly-devised program. Every church leader knows of times when carefully planned evangelistic programs have failed miserably, while God has brought exciting results from unexpected sources.

This fact, however, should not cause us to quit planning effective and aggressive evangelistic strategies. It simply reminds us to rely heavily on God's grace instead of human ingenuity. It reminds us to be flexible and daring in our varied attempts to reach people for Christ. "Sow your seed in the morning, and at evening let not your hands be idle, for you do not know which will succeed, whether this or that, or whether both will do equally well" (Eccl 11:6).

Here, then, are some basic principles for graceful harvesting.

1. *Every Church Member a Receiver of Grace*

You cannot give away what you do not have. Successful harvesters must first receive and experience the grace of God in their own lives. Jesus came to give abundant life, and to give "one blessing after another" from the fullness of His grace (John 1:16, 10:10). Many Christians, unfortunately, have never learned to really accept and live in the fullness and forgiveness of His grace.

We raised pigs on my parents' farm. Twice a year, baby pigs were born in our hog house. They lived the first few months of their lives on a fenced-in concrete slab. When the pigs were old enough to be weaned, we opened the gates so they could run out into the pasture field. Amazingly, though, even when the gate was open, the pigs would remain on the concrete slab for awhile, unaware of their new liberty. Eventually a few would cautiously paw their way over to the gate and, with some prodding from their owners, the pigs finally walked into the green grass of freedom!

Amazingly, some Christians seem unaware of the wonderful freedom grace brings. Until we personally accept the grace of God, we remain penned in by a fence that God has graciously torn down, imprisoned by bars His Son died to remove. We are like the prodigal son starving as the slave of a pig-farmer, when we could be at home with our Father. Why live in sin's pigpen when you could be feasting on God's grace? Or as the apostle Paul put it, "Are you so foolish? After beginning with the Spirit, are you now trying to attain your goal by human effort?" (Gal 3:3).

2. Every Church Member a Giver of Grace

To be effective in God's harvest field, every member of Christ's church needs to heed Paul's words in Colossians 4:5-6: "Be wise in the way you act toward outsiders; make the most of every opportunity. Let your conversation be *always full of grace*, seasoned with salt, so that you may know how to answer everyone" (italics mine). Like salt added to food, a believer's gracious words and deeds can create thirst for the things of God.

On November 9, 1965, the largest power failure in history blacked out parts of nine northeastern states, including nearly all of New York City. Railroads and subways ground to a halt, stranding more than a million travelers. The next day, the headline on the front page of the *New York Times* read, "City Gropes in Dark," and a photo of stranded subway passengers carried the caption, "On a Train Going Nowhere."

But farther down on the same page, a smaller headline read, "Miss Liberty Shines Through Blackout." Drawing on electricity from a New Jersey power plant, the Statue of Liberty's floodlit base and lighted torch had remained illuminated throughout the blackout. The article noted, "Except for an occasional passing river craft, the statue appeared to be the only beacon of light in the harbor."[2]

Many of our friends and neighbors are groping in the dark. For them, life is like riding a train going nowhere.

Believers in Christ, however, have a power source that enables us to keep shining in the darkness. There are times when we are the only beacon of light our friends will ever see. The Lord counts on us to be His grace-givers and His light-bringers.

3. Every Problem an Opportunity for Grace

It is important not to allow church problems to immobilize us or distract us from the harvest. The book of Ecclesiastes warns, "Whoever watches the wind will not plant; whoever looks at the clouds will not reap" (Eccl 11:4). If we look hard enough, we can always find some excuse for failure, some justification for inactivity, some reason why conditions are less than ideal for harvesting.

Problems, however, are simply opportunities for God's grace to function. Problems are reminders of human inadequacy, and thus compel us to grow gracefully when we might otherwise sit complacently.

Sometimes we are confronted with difficult choices. Church leaders wrestle daily with problems which have no easy answers. Sometimes we do not know which way to turn. We can identify with the comical advice of Yogi Berra, who urged, "When you come to a crossroads, *take* it!"

Crossroads in ministry are opportunities for God to manifest His grace. In 1 Corinthians 16:8-9, Paul expressed his intention to continue ministering in Ephesus a little longer, "because a great door for effective work has opened to me, and there are many who oppose me." Despite the problems, he saw opportunities for effective work. Open doors and obstinate opposition often go together. We need to recognize the gracious possibilities which usually come mingled with perplexing problems.

4. Every Task Undertaken with Grace

1 Samuel 13:19 tells us, "Not a blacksmith could be found in the whole land of Israel." This was a major crisis in an agricultural society which depended on blacksmiths to forge and sharpen farm tools. It was also a time of hand-to-hand combat; soldiers depended on blacksmiths to form and sharpen their swords and spears. Somehow, Israel's shrewd rivals, the Philistines, managed to eliminate the blacksmith's trade in Israel. Though the Bible does tell us the details, apparently the blacksmiths were either killed, captured, or forced to stop practicing their craft.

The result were disastrous. Where did the Israelites have to go to have their tools sharpened? To their arch-enemies, the Philistines! "So all Israel went down to the Philistines to have their plowshares, mattocks, axes and sickles sharpened. The price was two thirds of a shekel for sharpening plowshares and mattocks, and a third of a shekel for sharpening forks and axes and for repointing goads" (1 Sam 13:20-21).

With their blacksmiths gone, the Israelites suffered *humiliation*. (They had to swallow their pride each time they sought the services of a Philistine blacksmith.) They suffered *financial hardship*. (The Philistines, of course, charged exorbitant prices.) But the most serious consequence was this: "So on the day of battle not a soldier with Saul and Jonathan had a sword or spear in his hand; only Saul and his son Jonathan had them" (1 Sam 13:22). There were only two swords in the whole land, and these were owned by the king and his son!

The soldiers of Israel were virtually unarmed, all because there were no *blacksmiths*. These unheralded servants worked behind the scenes in sweaty, dusty, out-of-the-way shops. But the army of God could not fight without them.

God's army still needs "blacksmiths," people who serve gracefully and consistently behind the scenes. In every congregation, there are countless difficult and thankless tasks which must be done. Servants of Christ seldom receive praise for repairing the church furnace, cleaning the church restrooms, washing the communion cups, or calling on disgruntled members. Such jobs are seldom even noticed, until they are left undone!

The whole army of Israel suffered when their humble blacksmiths disappeared. Similarly, the graceful church cannot afford to take for granted those who do "blacksmith" jobs: the secretary who carefully types and prints the weekly bulletin, the Sunday School teacher who thoughtfully prepares her lesson, the youth sponsor who gives up his day off to chaperon a teenage outing, the musician who spends Saturday in an empty sanctuary preparing inspiring music for Sunday's service, the baby-sitter who changes diapers in the church nursery while the rest of the congregation enjoys a special program.

Much of God's work takes place behind the scenes. The upfront and noticeable soldiers in God's army depend heavily on the less visible but equally vital workers who keep the tools sharp.

I thank God for people willing to tackle unglamorous jobs with grace and dedication. I thank God for Christians committed enough to get their hands dirty, tough enough to work up a sweat, humble enough to serve without recognition, reliable enough to pitch in whenever needed.

I thank God for blacksmiths.

5. Every Gathering an Expression of Grace

Graceful churches put a high priority on worship. When you attend their assemblies, you find them doing things that help people worship "in spirit and truth" (John 4:24). Graceless churches, on the other hand, show serious deficiencies in worship; services are dull, lifeless, and predictable, with little of the joy and vitality which should characterize people gathered in the presence of a gracious God.

The primary purpose of corporate worship is always to honor God. As C. S. Lewis has written:

> . . . As long as you notice, and have to count, the steps, you are not yet dancing but only learning to dance. A good shoe is a shoe you don't notice. Good reading becomes possible when you need not consciously think about eyes, or light, or print, or spelling. The perfect church service would be one we were almost unaware of; our attention would have been on God.[3]

In graceful churches, every gathering is a time to encounter the gracious God who has drawn us near to Himself through Jesus Christ. We cannot help but be a "visitor friendly" church when we understand how God lovingly opened His arms to us "while we were still sinners" (Rom 5:5). Before church growth experts began designing "seeker sensitive" worship services, God Himself demonstrated the ultimate in seeker sensitivity: "He rewards those who earnestly seek Him" (Heb 11:6).

Any time believers spend together should be a "grace period," a time when God's grace is welcomed and celebrated. This is true not only of corporate worship services, but also the other occasions when Christians assemble. God calls us to act gracefully whether we are meeting to resolve church problems (Acts 6:1-6), to talk about offerings and finances (2 Cor 8:7, 9:8), or to deal with matters of church discipline (Matt 18:12-20). Small groups need to be graceful gatherings where seekers find love and acceptance.

Christian families need to express the love of God through hospitality — turning our homes into "hospitals" which administer healing grace.[4] The healthy relationships modeled in a Christian home can break down barriers to the gospel. As Joseph Aldrich has observed:

> The two greatest forces in evangelism are a healthy church and a healthy marriage. The two are interdependent. You can't have one without the other. It is the healthy marriage, however, which is the 'front lines weapon.' The Christian family in a community is the ultimate evangelistic tool, assuming the home circle is an open one in which the beauty of the gospel is readily available. It's the old story: *when love is seen, The message is heard.*[5]

SUMMARY

When Jesus looked upon the crowds, He saw a harvest of hurting people who were like sheep without a shepherd. The church must reach out to these lost sheep with compassion and grace.

One of the marvels of God's grace is that He uses imperfect people to accomplish His perfect will. This is true even in the urgent work of harvesting souls. Earl Palmer illustrates it well:

> In the Bay Area where I live, I sometimes make jokes at the expense of a small town called Milpitas. Once while speaking on radio, I said, 'You know, Beethoven is not on trial when the Milpitas Junior High Orchestra plays the Ninth Symphony. And Jesus Christ is not on trial when you or I or even C.S. Lewis tries to express the faith in a conversation or a sermon.'
>
> Then about a year later it occurred to me: But were it not for the Milpitas Junior High Orchestra — who would hear Beethoven? Even if badly played, it is better than no playing at all. Who plays Beethoven perfectly?

Some people trudge from church to church looking for the perfect rendition. They'll never find it.

W. H. Auden once observed that even though the line is smudged, we can read the line, and that is the mystery of evangelism: even though we smudge the line, it can still be read. You can whistle the tune of the Ninth Symphony even after listening in the Milpitas gymnasium.[6]

We will never reach out perfectly. There will always be plenty of room for improvement in our evangelism efforts. But if we speak the good news with authenticity and grace, we will eventually experience the joys of the harvest. As Jesus said, "Even now the reaper draws his wages, even now he harvests the crop for eternal life, so that the sower and the reaper may be glad together" (John 4:36).

The harvest is ready. We must find a way to help.

NOTES: CHAPTER FOUR

[1]Kenton K. Smith, editor, *Mark* (Cincinnati: Standard Publishing, 1968), pp. 35-36.

[2]*The New York Times*, November 10, 1965, p. 1.

[3]C.S. Lewis, *Letters to Malcolm: Chiefly on Prayer* (New York: Harcourt Brace Janovich, 1963), p. 4.

[4]See my article, "Calling in Reverse," in *Christian Standard*, October 17, 1982.

[5]Joseph C. Aldrich, *Life-Style Evangelism* (Portland, OR: Multnomah, 1981), pp. 20-21.

[6]Earl Palmer, "Evangelism Takes Time," *Leadership*, Volume V, Spring 1984, p. 23.

5

GOD'S GRACE AND THE CHURCH GROWTH MOVEMENT

Several years ago, I read an article in which the author listed what he called "objections to church growth." What a strange topic! Why would anyone object to the growth of the church?

Of course, the devil would object, and non-Christians might object. In fact, the church in the book of Acts faced serious opposition from a wide range of adversaries who objected to church growth. Religious leaders (Acts 5:27-29, 8:1-3), government officials (Acts 12:1), and even businessmen (Acts 19:23-28) all opposed the expansion of Christ's church for one reason or another.

But it seems very odd indeed when objections to church growth flow from the lips and pens of sincere believers. Does not every Christian long to see Christ's church expand? Does not every child of God pray for the day when "the earth will be filled with the knowledge of the glory of the Lord, as the waters cover the sea" (Hab 2:14)?

The root of the problem, however, really is not church growth, which dedicated believers everywhere earnestly desire.[1] The difficulty comes with certain perceptions and concerns regarding church growth as a movement.

In recent years, the church growth movement has poured forth a seemingly endless flow of books, articles, and seminars filled with practical advice for church leaders. Many good ideas have been brought into the public arena, and a number of helpful principles have been identified which are transferable to churches in any culture. In a real sense, God's people owe a debt of gratitude to the church growth pioneers who have spurred us on to love and good works in fulfilling Christ's Great Commission.

At times, however, church growth concepts have been misapplied and misdirected into an unhealthy "growthism" which distorts or overlooks important Scriptural principles and leads to burnout instead of blessing for Christian leaders. Even churches which appear healthy are sometimes led by preachers who privately confess to a serious imbalance in their lives. They passionately want their churches to grow; but at the same time, they do not want to sacrifice their families, their theological integrity, and their personal health on the altar of so-called "success."

The purpose of this chapter, therefore, is not to point fingers of blame, but to persuade both the critics and the adherents of the church growth movement to join hands in a common struggle for doctrinal accuracy and effective methods. As a church-planter and teacher, it is my goal to offer a friendly and fair-minded critique of the church growth movement from the perspective of a co-laborer and fellow-struggler. I believe it is possible to achieve a healthy harmonization of church growth principles, Biblical truth, and personal wholeness, without shortchanging or discarding any of the above.

THE HAZARDS OF GROWTHISM

By "growthism," I mean any unbalanced preoccupation with church growth (especially numerical growth) which harms churches and their leaders. Robert M. Woods introduces this term in an article entitled,

"Church Growthism: The New Heresy?" He warns:

> Is it possible that a new 'ism' is developing in our congregations? The 'ism' that I am referring to is growthism. This is the philosophy that we must grow at any cost, doing whatever it takes to get bigger.[2]

Instead of growing gracefully, growthism means growing dangerously.

As in any healthy organism, growth is a normal and healthy condition for the church. Non-growth is abnormal. Growth must be the expected and desired condition for Christ's church (see Appendix Two, page 211).

Nevertheless, normal growth takes place in a framework of balance. God gave the human body two eyes, two ears, two feet, two hands. These parts of the body function together in harmony and grow at approximately the same rate. If one leg is considerably longer than the other, the body experiences serious problems of balance.

Jesus said He would build His church upon the solid rock of His Son's identity as the Son of God. Christ is a Master Builder. He does not throw a few stones together, hastily and haphazardly slapping them with mortar. Piece by piece, section by section, in perfect balance, the Lord fits all the parts together until they form a holy temple (Eph 2:19-22).

Of course, growth sometimes occurs in surprising spurts; and churches, like adolescent children, go through awkward stages. But genuine church growth is an ongoing process of "attaining to the whole measure of the fullness of Christ" (Eph 4:13).

Growth is not a problem; it is the desired end. But wild, unrestrained growth is not desirable; it is cancerous. Healthy growth is theologically sound and emotionally exhilarating. Unhealthy growthism, on the other hand, is theologically and emotionally hazardous.

We need to find a balanced approach which is both *biodegradable* (when you boil it down, it is consistent with life), and *Bible-degradable* (when you boil it down, it is consistent with *Scripture*).

In order to keep marching forward, we need to identify and avoid the land-mines Satan tries to place in our path.

Theological Hazards

One danger could be termed *plastic theology*. The Greek word *plastos* originally described something soft and pliable, easily shaped and molded. It is used once in the New Testament, in 2 Peter 2:3, where Peter warns about teachers who exploit people with "plastic" stories they have made up or fabricated.

A few years ago, I read a news item about some enterprising Japanese farmers who developed a unique new fruit they called "cubic watermelons." The melons tasted exactly like ordinary melons. The only difference was, these melons were square-shaped, which made them easy to ship and easy for consumers to store in their refrigerators. How did the farmers make a cubic watermelon? It was easy. As the fruit began to develop, the growers placed it into a special square box, and the fruit simply grew into the shape of its surroundings.

Plastic theology does the same thing. Though Scripture warns, "Do not be conformed any longer to the pattern of this world" (Rom 12:2), today's church faces tremendous pressure to compromise the gospel of grace in order to please the crowd. Lacking a firm anchor in Scriptural truth, plastic theology bends with every wind of teaching.

An anonymous critic expressed this concern in the following note which appeared on a seminary bulletin board:

The Baby-Boomers Translation of Acts 2:42:

> And they continued occasionally in portions of the apostles' doctrine, along with ideas from non-traditionalists, and in a type of fellowship that doesn't include taking an offering because seekers shouldn't be asked to contribute, and in the breaking of bread in a side room so as not to embarrass the unchurched, and in prayer, not necessarily directed to God or in the name of Jesus in order that no one be offended.

Os Guinness bluntly charges that the church growth movement has a theological understanding which is "superficial, with almost no element of biblical criticism."[3] William J. Abraham laments what he calls "a serious lack of theological balance" in the church growth movement, noting that "competing and even conflicting doctrinal traditions have been able to embrace church growth theory without shedding any theological tears."[4] According to Abraham,

> What we have is considerable theological disarray, shallowness, or indifference, a fostering of false hopes concerning what can be achieved by research and programming, and a rather conspicuous failure to face up to the radical demands of the Christian gospel.[5]

Plastic theology is no substitute for the rock-solid truth of God.

Another hazard is *pragmatic theology*. In fairness, no responsible spokesman for the church growth movement actually advocates replacing Biblical truth with a philosophy which says bluntly, "If it works, do it." However, the movement unashamedly urges leaders to be aggressively pragmatic. Further, church growth conferences repeatedly reinforce the notion that theologians and seminaries are out of touch with the practical realities of day to day ministry. To an extent, this charge may be true.

At the same time, however, it misses the point. Whether or not certain *theologians* are out of touch, there is a grave danger in concluding that *theology* is out of touch. If God is real and His Word is true, then there is nothing more needed — and nothing more practical — than healthy theology. Of course it must be presented in lively, clear, helpful, creative ways which communicate authentically to today's audiences; nonetheless, we still need theology.

A few years ago, I conducted a leadership seminar in Port-au-Prince, Haiti. For eight or nine hours a day, I led a verse-by-verse study of the book of 1 Peter with the help of an interpreter who translated my lectures into the Creole language.

I was amazed at the Haitians' commitment to learning the Word. Many of my listeners were desperately poor in terms of material possessions, but they possessed a strong sense of the practical value of Scripture. One man rose before dawn every day and rode his bicycle fourteen miles in order to study with us. All of the participants listened to me for hours while sitting on hard wooden benches, taking notes in small notebooks on their laps. When I offered to give the students a break or to finish early, they insisted, through the interpreter: "Continue!"

American Christians have many material possessions, but our culture is becoming increasingly impoverished in terms of spiritual depth. Biblical illiteracy is rampant, and people cannot apply in their lives what they do not know. Countless American churches need to be "Bereanized" — that is, they need to adopt the hungry attitude of the believers in Berea who "received the message with great eagerness and examined the Scriptures every day" (Acts 17:11). We need to experience a renewal of the kind of attitude expressed in Psalm 119:97: "Oh, how I love your law!" As Peter wrote, "Like newborn babies, crave pure spiritual milk, so that by it you may grow up in your salvation, now that you have tested that the Lord is good" (1 Pet 2:2-3).

Rightly understood, Biblical theology *is* pragmatic. God's truth works! "All Scripture," Paul wrote, "is God breathed *and is useful* . . ." (2 Tim 3:16, italics mine). Doctrine (the word simply means "teaching") does not have to be dry, dull, and irrelevant. *Sound* doctrine promotes the health of the church (Titus 1:9, 2:1). In fact, the word translated "sound" (Greek *hugiaino*) literally meant *healthy* or *whole*. Luke, who was a physician, used the same word in Luke 5:31, where Jesus says, "It is not those who are *well* [healthy, sound] who need a physician, but those who are sick." In any culture, people still hunger for the healthy, satisfying message of the Bible which offers practical help for leading an informed life of faith.[6]

The apostle Paul certainly recognized no dichotomy between theology and the issues of real life. A familiar pattern emerges in his letters. Paul first establishes a doctrinal foundation (as in Ephesians chapters one through three), then explains the practical application (as in Ephesians chapters four through six).[7]

It is possible for dangerous imbalances to occur in either direction. Theology without practice dissolves into aimless theorizing; practicality without a theological base leads to a shallow pop spirituality far removed from the life-changing message of Jesus.

William Abraham comments:

In itself there is nothing at all wrong with a healthy commitment to develop policies and practices in evangelism that really do achieve intentionally adopted goals. What is at issue is the way this spirit begins to corrupt various aspects of evangelism. . . . Unless we are very careful such delicate matters as friendship and love will be turned into one more utilitarian means or tool to increase the statistics of church membership. Before we know what is happening sacred human relationships will have lost their integrity and the distinctive character of Christian love will have been eroded by an evangelistic orientation that construes them not as ends in themselves but as means to an end.[8]

In his book, *Mere Christianity*, C. S. Lewis compares theology to a map:

> . . . a vague religion — all about feeling God in nature, and so on — is so attractive. It is all thrills and no work; like watching the waves from the beach. But you will not get to Newfoundland by studying the Atlantic that way, and you will not get eternal life by simply feeling the presence of God in flowers or music. Neither will you get anywhere by looking at maps without going to sea. Nor will you be very safe if you go to sea without a map.
> In other words, theology is practical: especially now. In the old days, when there was less education and discussion, perhaps it was possible to get on with a very few simple ideas about God. But it is not so now. Everyone reads, everyone hears things discussed. Consequently, if you do not listen to theology, that will not mean that you have no ideas about God. It will mean that you have a lot of wrong ones — bad, muddled, out-of-date ideas.[9]

Another theological hazard is *pluralistic theology*. Pluralism is the worldview, increasingly common in our time, which embraces more than one ultimate reality. In his book, *The Gospel in a Pluralist Society*, Leslie Newbigin offers a helpful distinction between cultural and religious pluralism:

> Cultural pluralism I take to be the attitude which welcomes the variety of different cultures and lifestyles within one society and believes that this is an enrichment of human life. I accept the truth of this . . . . Religious pluralism, on the other hand, is the belief that the differences between the religions are not a matter of

84

truth and falsehood, but of different perceptions of the one truth; that to speak of religious belief as true or false is inadmissible. Religious belief is a private matter. Each of us is entitled to have — as we say — a faith of our own. This is religious pluralism, and it is a widely held opinion in contemporary British society.[10]

One cannot escape the impression that religious pluralism is fast becoming the "politically correct" view of spirituality on college and university campuses in North America. It leads to a nonchalant acceptance of divergent or even conflicting views as equally valid. The prevelance of this attitude helps explain the widespread acceptance in our culture of what I call "popular universalism," which will be discussed at length in the next chapter.

God calls us to interact dynamically with our culture and present Christ to our contemporaries. The danger is that in our zeal to reach people, we will fail to help them recognize Christianity's distinctive truth-claims. As Robert Woods explains, "Christians should understand the values, ideas, and culture in which we live. We do not do this to accommodate and sell out, but to equip us to speak boldly against the lies of that culture."[11]

To an extent, a "target audience" of non-Christians may help to shape a church's methodology. But there is great danger when the target audience shapes a church's theology. Harvie Conn asks:

Recognizing the importance of our audience, can we develop a genuine sensitivity to the needs of people without drifting toward a Madison Avenue philosophy of public relations? Will God become only our "great felt-need meeter" in the sky? Can we develop a concern for itches without catering to people with "itching ears" (2 Tim. 4:3)?[12]

In an atmosphere of cultural pluralism, the church must point to the uniqueness of Jesus Christ. We must know the facts and defend our faith with gracious firmness.

One of the most destructive theological hazards which threatens the church leader is simply *performance theology*. Even while outwardly repudiating the idea of salvation by works and insisting on a solid theology of grace, many leaders still fall into the performance trap.

David Seamands writes:

> Many feel if only they could achieve success in some area of their work, they would prove themselves to be worthwhile. Then they would be accepted and loved by God and others, and therefore feel better about themselves. So they work harder, perform better, and may even achieve a high measure of success, only to discover that *no amount of doing or achieving* can change how they inwardly feel about themselves.[13]

I identify with this struggle. I have had high expectations of myself my whole life. I hate to waste time. I tend to overplan my days, even filling my days off with lists of jobs to accomplish. I have even found myself envying the way God "never slumbers or sleeps," because I could get so much more done if I did not have to spend several hours in bed every night!

Many of my role models in ministry, though godly and capable men, have inadvertently reinforced my performance-oriented tendencies. It did not take long for me to learn that the preachers I respected most were typically working 80 hours per week. One of my respected mentors used to say, "A preacher should even *walk* fast to show people your enthusiasm."

The problem has been intensified by my deep inner longing to make my life count for God. I sincerely want to do whatever it takes to reach people for Christ, and I want to challenge my congregation to live out our faith at the highest level of excellence. To paraphrase Barry Goldwater, I have tried to convince myself that "Workaholism in the pursuit of church growth is no vice."

Nevertheless, good intentions aside, we highly driven and performance-oriented church leaders need to reevaluate what we are communicating to our congregations. Are our sermons, newsletter articles, and our personal example sending the message that one's relationship with God depends on our performance rather than on grace? Are we really growing gracefully, or just performing impressively?

David Johnson and Jeff Van Vonderen sum up the danger of performance theology as follows:

> A spiritual load is placed upon the people by a theology that says, "God is adding up all your good behaviors and all your bad behaviors. If, in the end, the good outweighs the bad, He might accept you into His heaven" . . . . The only hope you have in this system is that your good behaviors outweigh your bad — but the operative word here is "weigh." You carry it all.
> . . . In a performance-based system, you will be the bearer of the burden. In a grace-based system, you will be constantly directed to Jesus as your only hope, encouraged to rest in Him as your only source of life and power.[14]

Emotional Hazards

Ministry, of course, has always carried with it some emotional hazards. The apostle Paul spoke of the daily pressure he felt because of his concern for the churches. His intense passion for God's people caused him pain even when, technically, the responsibility was not his own: "Who is weak, and I do not feel weak? Who is led into sin, and I do not inwardly burn?" (2 Cor 11:28-29).

Both Scripture and common sense tell us there is a close positive relationship between strong leadership and church growth. The church growth movement especially highlights the role of the senior minister. C. Peter Wagner writes, "In America, the primary catalytic factor for growth in a local church is the pastor."[15] According to Lyle Schaller,

> The pastor must want that congregation to grow. The pastor must have a strong future-orientation. The pastor must be able to see opportunities where others see problems and conflicts. The pastor must be willing to accept and fill a strong leadership role and serve as the number-one leader in that congregation.[16]

Unfortunately, good people are burning themselves out and sometimes destroying both their health and their families while trying to prove successful in this incredibly demanding task of leading a church.[17] Could it be that a misapplication of church growth principles actually contributes to the growing problem of burnout among Christian leaders? The church growth movement correctly calls us to excellence and effectiveness in ministry; but in some circles the emphasis is on human effort rather than growing gracefully. A mentality which puts enormous emphasis on measurable results can easily feed the unhealthy drivenness of the many leaders whose perfectionistic tendencies lead them to think, "I would rather burn out than rust out or cop out!" As D. G. Kehl says:

> Ironically, Christian believers are especially susceptible to burnout. This is true for a number of reasons. First, the possibility of burnout exists only where there is fire. . . . Our dedication to carrying out the Great Commission makes us cause oriented and goal oriented. Our intense desire to "make a difference for Christ," to "help change the world for God," makes us prime candidates for burnout if we see no results or only negligible ones.[18]

Why are ministers so vulnerable to the emotional hazards of growthism? Archibald Hart has identified several factors which produce significant stress:

1. Ministry is people-oriented, and many ministers have not been well-trained in dealing with conflict situations and difficult personalities; this is especially difficult since the church is a voluntary environment where people can choose to be, or not to be, involved.

2. Ministers often lack specific criteria for measuring the accomplishments of their work; it seems the work is never done; there is seldom a feeling of "closure."

3. Ministry often begins with unrealistic initial expectations, and young ministers are surprised by the many discouragements they encounter.

4. Ministry sometimes brings people into positions of high visibility (and even popularity), with the accompanying pitfalls of inflated personal pride and high congregational expectations.

5. Ministry places one's family on a pedestal too, and other family members may suffer from the stresses which come with high responsibility and visibility.[19]

Even in non-growing churches, ministers carry a heavy workload, struggle with the consequences of failure (since it seems that to fail in our job is to fail God), and often show a reluctance to seek help when feeling overwhelmed.

Many Christian leaders are literally "going for broke" as they try to help their churches grow.

Surely there is a better way.

WHERE IS BALANCE NEEDED?

Understanding Success and Failure

"Succeed" comes from a Latin word which meant to go up or to follow after, as when a king succeeds a previous monarch. No wonder we speak of "climbing up the ladder of success."

Americans tend to stress upward mobility. Ironically, Jesus defined greatness as *downward* mobility. "Whoever wants to become great among you must be your servant, and whoever wants to be first must be slave of all" (Mark 10:43-44).[20]

Interestingly, the word "success" rarely appears in the Bible. When it does, it usually is used to describe the blessings which result from courageous obedience to God's Word (Gen 39:23, Josh 1:3-9, 1 Chr 22:13, Ps 20:4, Prov 16:3). In fact, Scripture repeatedly challenges us to rethink our definitions of success.

SUCCESS IS *MORE* THAN . . .

Self-confidence, for God used people like Moses and Jeremiah who lacked confidence in their own abilities (Exod 4:10, Jer 1:6).

Good looks, for God used men like John the Baptist whose idea of "dressing for success" included rough leather belts and camels' hair suits (Mark 1:6).

Material wealth, for people like the rich young ruler possessed great riches yet "went away sad" instead of following Jesus (Mark 10:17-25).

Education, for despite his great wisdom and knowledge, Solomon recognized the futility and emptiness of learning as an end in itself (Eccl 1:12-18).

Physical strength, for God used Timothy despite his frequent illnesses, and He used Paul despite his repulsive and persistent thorn in the flesh (2 Cor 12:7-9, Gal 4:13-14, 1 Tim 5:23).

Popularity, for courageous prophets like Amos successfully fulfilled their mission by proclaiming a truthful though unpopular message (Amos 6:1-7).

Results, for Jesus successfully did God's will even when the crowds abandoned Him (John 6:66-69); on the other hand, even though Moses got results when he struck the rock and water came out, from God's viewpoint Moses had failed since he had been told to speak to the rock instead (Num 20:6-12).[21]

Success is finding God's will and doing it. "There is no wisdom, no insight, no plan that can succeed against the Lord" (Proverbs 21:30). The church growth movement correctly reminds us to ruthlessly examine our effectiveness in getting the job done. But churches large and small need to remember: real success cannot be measured simply by the number of people who attend a worship service or by the size of a church's buildings or budget.

A Christian definition of success might look more like this:

SUCCESS IS . . .

S *ervice*, for Jesus calls His people to wash the feet of others (Mark 10:45, John 13:14-17).

U *nselfishness*, for love expresses itself in committed concern for the wellbeing of others (1 Cor 13:4-6, Phil 2:3-4).

C *ontentment*, for true success comes when we learn to accept and celebrate whatever God has provided (Phil 4:11-13, 1 Tim 6:6-11).

C *ourage*, "for God did not give us a spirit of timidity, but a spirit of power, of love and of self-discipline" (2 Tim 1:7).

E *ndurance*, for faithfulness is a consistent lifelong willingness to follow Christ no matter what the outcome, a tenacious determination to persevere even through tough times (Luke 9:61-62, 2 Tim 6:6-8, Rev 2:10).

S *tewardship*, making the most of the opportunities God has granted to us, achieving our maximum potential as individuals and as congregations, while recognizing God has not granted everyone exactly the same gifts and opportunities (Matt 25:14-30, 1 Cor 4:2, Col 4:5, 1 Pet 4:10-11).

S *alvation*, for ultimately success cannot be defined by any earthly accomplishment but by God's gracious provision of eternal life through Christ (1 Cor 15:57-58, Eph 2:8-10).

Even when we correctly define success, it is still

hard to measure up. Sometimes, honest self-evaluation reveals selfishness, discontent, and fear in our hearts. Clearly, we are imperfect stewards, unworthy servants. Does this mean we are *failures*? Only if we forget God's grace! Real success depends upon a recognition of God's strength and grace in our times of personal weakness (2 Cor 12:9-10).

Archibald Hart offers a helpful perspective on failure:

> To be free to exercise your gifts and be fully what God intends you to be, you must face one solid reality of this world: Some failure is inevitable. And you cannot let your fear of failure stifle your creativity and freedom if you are going to be successful.
>
> . . . *Failure is for growing*. . . . Failure gives you the best feedback you need so that corrective adjustments can be made. Most scientists know this. They will concede that the best research they can perform is 90 per cent failure, 9 per cent luck, and 1 per cent planned success. The 90 per cent is very important. It helps them to plan for the next success. It leads the way to the next step. Without it there would be no more progress.[22]

Maintaining Commitment While Experiencing Contentment

According to comedian Henny Youngman, the shortest will ever written said simply, "Being of sound mind, I spent all my money!"

Since we have only one life to spend, it makes sense to invest ourselves fully in the things of God. Christ calls us to a commitment of self-denial — to save our lives by losing our lives for His sake (Mark 8:34-36). We must ask an important question, however: can churches and their leaders experience genuine contentment even while paying the price for dynamic growth?

The answer is "yes" if we are willing to grow gracefully. We can rest contentedly in the security of God's grace even as we move aggressively into the future. William H. Cook says we must choose the right definition of contentment. Contentment does *not* mean, "I should have my desires limited to what I already have, and that which I have already achieved." It means, "I should have my desires limited to that which I am convinced God wants me to have, and that which God wants me to achieve." Cook says, "There's a world of difference in those two ideas of contentment! The first spells laziness, the second spells lordship! Christian contentment majors on the lordship of Christ."[23]

Combining Strong Leadership with Personal Accountability

Capable leadership is a key to church growth, but unhealthy growthism occurs when leaders are accountable to no one. Like Diotrephes (3 John verse 9), egocentric, power-hungry, authoritarian leaders abuse their followers. Some well-meaning leaders go to the other extreme. They care so deeply about their people, they try to accept the impossible role of community rescuer and problem-solver. This leads only to burnout.

In a growing church, leadership *development* is the proper aim, not leadership *dominance*. The preacher can occupy a strong role of influence without allowing the congregation to become either a personality cult or a one-man-show.

Ideally, all leaders need to have not only a few "Timothies" (younger disciples they are seeking to develop), but also several "Barnabases" (faithful co-laborers who offer consistent encouragement and accountability), and at least one or two "Pauls" (mature mentors who can offer seasoned advice and correction).

Achieving Growth Both in Quantity and Quality

Critics of church growth often complain that an

emphasis on numerical growth leads to a loss of spiritual depth. The distinction between quantitative and qualitative growth, however, is artificial and misleading.

To illustrate this point, I often ask the students in my church growth class to consider a simple question: "Which would you rather have defending your city — either 100 poorly-trained police officers, or ten well-trained police officers?" After a bit of discussion, I explain that a community would be well advised to stop thinking in such "either/or" terms! One hundred poorly trained officers would be unsatisfactory; but neither should we be satisfied with a mere handful of well-trained officers. If it were up to me, I would prefer to have *100 **well**-trained police officers* defending our city!

Likewise, our goal in church growth is not to have 100 weak and shallow Christians; nor is it to have ten strong and deep ones! The only aim consistent with Christ's Great Commission is to develop as *many* as we can as *deeply* as we can.

The New Testament church managed to combine sound doctrine with explosive church growth (Acts 2:36-47).

We can too.

Blending Goal-Orientation with Grace-Orientation

Describing what he calls "Grace and God's Giants," William Cook writes:

> People who have power with God are not afraid of goals. They thrive on them. God apparently has no fear of them — He assigns them.
>
> Abraham's goal was to follow God anywhere, to the end of the earth if necessary, and gather people around him who would walk by faith. Moses' goal was to rescue all the Jews from bondage and lead them toward the Promised Land. David's goal was to save his people from the Philistines, even if he had to fight Goliath himself. Elijah's goal was to destroy Baal worship in Israel. No

risk was too great, no odds too big. Elisha's goal was to have a double portion of the spirit and power of Elijah resting upon him, and he would not be denied. Christ's goal — he stated it in two ways — "For the Son of man is come to seek and to save that which is lost" (Luke 19:10), and "I am come that they might have life, and that they might have it more abundantly" (John 10:10).[24]

The kind of goal-orientation often mentioned in church growth circles is healthy as long as it causes us to depend more fully on the grace and power of God.

Max Lucado relates his personal experience with grace-oriented goals:

> Failure taught me to pray. . . .
> Prayer only makes sense when you have quit trying to do ministry yourself. I've learned that as things go smoothly, I pray less. As our goals shrink, I pray less. As things become more manageable, I pray less. But as we reach out, stretch ourselves, and tackle God-sized dreams, I pray more.[25]

Balancing Timeless Truths with Timely Methods

God's Word sets forth timeless principles which are relevant in any culture and in any generation. Acts 2:42, for example, summarizes four ongoing and non-negotiable emphases: the apostles' teaching, fellowship, breaking of bread, and prayer. However, Scripture also endorses the thoughtful use of methods which communicate the truth to differing audiences in timely and relevant ways (Acts 20:20-21, 1 Cor 9:19-23).[26]

Every autumn, I marvel at the multicolored foliage on the trees. The different shades of orange, brown, red, and yellow display God's ability to produce beauty through change. What often goes overlooked, however, is that the bulk of the tree (the roots, trunk, limbs, and bark) remain basically the same season after season — growing slowly, unglamorously, almost imperceptibly.

The roots and trunk are not very colorful, but they provide the stability necessary for the leaves to change with the seasons.

A tree displays God's beautiful blending of *that which changes* with *that which does **not** change*. Similarly, a healthy church maintains strong roots in the timeless and unchanging truths of God (Col 2:6-8), while displaying a colorful and attractive adaptability and timeliness in every season.

SUMMARY

Like an alarm clock stubbornly ringing out its wake up call, the church growth movement demands our attention and compels us to focus on the urgent task of disciple-making.

God provides the resources so we can accomplish this task without either departing from Biblical truth or burning ourselves out.

If we are to make wise use of church growth principles, we must re-learn the lesson any farmer knows. It is important to plow, plant, and harvest wisely — but ultimately, it is God who makes things grow (1 Cor 3:7).

NOTES: CHAPTER FIVE

[1]Of course, there are many professing Christians who resist growth simply because of the changes and discomforts growth may bring. It is easy to give lip service to the need for evangelism and missions, but many are unwilling to make the personal and congregational adjustments necessary. As C. Peter Wagner and others have stated, we must be willing to "pay the price" for growth.

[2]Robert M. Woods, "Church Growthism: The New Heresy?" *The Restoration Herald*, July, 1992, p. 8.

[3]Os Guinness, "Church Growth — Weaknesses to Watch," Part II, *Table Talk*, February, 1992, p. 52.

[4]William J. Abraham, *The Logic of Evangelism* (Grand Rapids: Eerdmans, 1989), p. 80.

[5]*Ibid.*, p. 81.

[6]Scripture identifies many positive and practical results of teaching Biblical doctrine: (1) it helps to guide the young (Deut 11:19, Ps 119:9, 2 Tim 2:15); (2) it helps to establish and strengthen the faith of new believers (Acts 11:26, Eph 4:14); (3) it provides a moral compass for discerning right from wrong (Heb 5:14); (4) it provides greater boldness and depth for the preacher (2 Tim 4:2); (5) it builds discernment for distinguishing important matters from trivial matters (1 Tim 1:4-6, Titus 3:8-9); (6) it leads to greater freedom in Christ (John 8:31-32).

[7]This same kind of pattern may be observed in Paul's letters to the Romans and Colossians.

[8]Abraham, *Logic of Evangelism*, p. 77.

[9]C.S. Lewis, *Mere Christianity*, New York: MacMillan, 1952, p. 136.

[10]Leslie Newbigin, *The Gospel in a Pluralist Society* (Grand Rapids: Eerdmans, 1989), p. 14.

[11]Robert M. Woods, "Church Growthism," p. 8.

[12]Harvie Conn, *Evangelism: Doing Justice and Preaching Grace* (Grand Rapids: Zondervan, 1982), p. 16.

[13]Seamands, *Healing Grace*, p. 160.

[14]David Johnson and Jeff Van Vonderen, *Spiritual Abuse*, pp. 150-151.

[15]C. Peter Wagner, *Your Church Can Grow*, p. 55.

[16]Lyle E. Schaller, *Growing Plans* (Nashville: Abingdon, 1983), p. 85.

[17]Members of all the so-called helping professions are vulnerable to burnout, and ministers are no exception. Occasional experiences of loss, frustration, and even depression may be accepted as a normal part of life. Burnout, however, goes deeper. People who are truly burned out feel a profound sense of physical and emotional exhaustion, and sometimes a devastating sense of spiritual emptiness as well. As Archibald Hart explains, "Whatever its specific

form, it generally leads to a progressive loss of ambition, idealism, energy, calling, and purpose." See Archibald Hart, "The Loss-Proneness of Ministry," *Minister's Personal Library Journal*, 1981, p. 3.

[18]D.G. Kehl, "Burnout: The Risk of Reaching Too High," *Christianity Today*, November 20, 1981, p. 26.

[19]Archibald Hart, "Loss-Proneness," pp. 4-6.

[20]See also Philippians 2:3-11.

[21]See also Matthew 7:21-23.

[22]Archibald Hart, *The Success Factor* (Pasadena, CA: Fuller Theological Seminary, 1984), p. 58.

[23]William H. Cook, *Success, Motivation, and the Scriptures* (Nashville: Broadman, 1974), pp. 128-129.

[24]*Ibid.*, pp. 133-134.

[25]Max Lucado, "The Applause of Heaven and Earth," *Leadership*, Vol. XIII, Summer, 1992, p. 19.

[26]For a fuller discussion of the "timeless" and "timely" aspects of the gospel, see Joe S. Ellis, *The Church on Purpose*, pp. 21-25.

6

CHILDREN OF A GRACEFUL GOD

The first verse of the Bible says, "In the beginning, God . . ." (Gen 1:1). The last verse of the Bible says, "The grace of the Lord Jesus be with God's people" (Rev 22:21). From cosmic creation to personal salvation, from Biblical theology to church growth, it all begins with God, and it all depends on grace.

If it is true that "to be always relevant, you have to say things which are eternal,"[1] the truth of God's grace will always be relevant. God sends the church into a world He created, to people He loves, on a mission He empowers, for a victory he guarantees. Our message is theocentric (God-centered).[2] We are children of "God our Father, who loved us and by His grace gave us eternal encouragement and good hope" (2 Thess 2:16).

God is the Great Initiator. Before He gave the Great Commission, God gave the Great Remission — forgiveness of our sins (Matt 26:26-28, Col 1:14).

God is the Cheerful Giver. Before we gave our hearts to Him, He gave His Son for us (Rom 5:6-8, 1 John 4:10).

God is the Only Savior. Before he asked us to go and make disciples, He opened His arms to us and graciously adopted us into His royal family (Eph 1:5-7).

God's amazing grace undergirds our life and growth as churches and as individuals. Before we can grow gracefully, we must understand our position as children of a graceful God.

GOD, THE GREAT INITIATOR

George W. Peters reminds us that God's willingness to intervene in the affairs of mankind comprises one of the great and distinctive doctrines of the Christian faith:

In Christianity God is the great and merciful Initiator. He reaches down to needy humanity. In all other religions of the world humans reach up in search for reality and salvation. The "But God" rings through in apostolic preaching. God broke through and entered history: He loved the world; He acted in the interest of the world; He sent His Son to procure salvation. God broke through on the day of Pentecost and poured out the Holy Spirit. Therefore the multitude on the day of Pentecost heard the apostles proclaim "the mighty deed of God" (Acts 2:11) and not the great discoveries or illuminations or intuitions or scientific insights of men.[3]

Occasionally I ask someone to do me a favor. I might ask my wife, one of my children, or a coworker to help perform a chore, lend me some change for the soda machine, or allow me some extra time to complete an assignment at work. My friends, family, and colleagues usually are glad to do me a favor, perhaps in part because they know I will one day return the favor to them. But how could I ever expect any favors from *God*? How could I ever ask the Lord of the universe to "do me a favor"? God owes us no favors. As God asked Job, "Who has a claim against me that I must pay? Everything under heaven belongs to me" (Job 41:11). As the apostle Paul asked, "Who has ever given to God, that God should repay him?" (Rom 11:35). The wonder of God's grace is that *God has done us a favor!* He has freely bestowed His unmerited favor upon us in Christ.[4]

A sign attached to a church building said it well: "You aren't too bad to come in, and you aren't too good to stay out."

As sinners, we deserve the condemnation of the law. "If you, O Lord, kept a record of sins, O Lord, who could stand?" (Ps 130:3). But on the cross, God took the initiative to remove our guilt and restore our relationship with Him. Jesus, the perfect lawkeeper, suffered the penalty we deserved as lawbreakers. "He Himself bore our sins in His body on the tree" (1 Pet 2:24).

Such graciousness is a rare commodity — difficult to understand, and even more difficult to practice in our lives. James Dobson relates the humorous irony of a sign which allegedly hung outside the halls of a convent. The sign read: "Absolutely no trespassing! Trespassers will be prosecuted to the fullest extent of the law!" (Signed, *Sisters of Mercy*).[5]

Throughout the Bible, however, God reveals a willingness to offer mercy and grace even to those who have trespassed against Him. He is the Great Initiator.

Grace in the Old Testament

Grace is not just a New Testament concept. Even in the book of Genesis, "Noah found favor (grace) in the eyes of the Lord," and Jacob told Esau, "The Lord has been gracious to me" (Gen 6:8, 33:11).

Several of the Psalms reveal God's wrath, but not without mention of His mercy: "For His anger last only a moment, but His favor lasts a lifetime; weeping may remain for a night, but rejoicing comes in the morning" (Ps 30:5). Others recount the marvel of forgiveness: "Blessed is he whose transgressions are forgiven, whose sins are covered" (Ps 32:1); "He does not treat us as our sins deserve or repay us according to our iniquities" (Ps 103:10). Still other Psalms praise God for the lavish love by which he blesses His people beyond all expectation (Ps 145:1-21).

Though often required to speak a harsh message of judgment, the prophets also spoke about grace. Jeremiah tells how God has loved His people with an everlasting love and has drawn them to Himself with loving kindness (Jeremiah 31:3). Hosea is a living parable of grace (Hos 2:23-3:1). Micah asks, "Who is a God like you, who pardons sin . . . ? You do not stay angry forever but delight to show mercy" (Micah 7:18-19). God even extended grace to people outside of Israel, like the widow of Zarephath and Naaman the Syrian (1 Kgs 17:7-24, 2 Kgs 5:1-19, Luke 4:25-27). When the hated Ninevites repented and God spared their city, unhappy Jonah complained in anger: "I knew that you are a gracious and compassionate God, slow to anger and abounding in love, a God who relents from sending calamity" (Jonah 4:2).

The story of David and Mephibosheth, a tender account tucked away in 2 Samuel chapter 9, illustrates the marvel of grace. Despite the fact that he was the son of Jonathan, and the only remaining descendant of the late King Saul, Mephibosheth was an unimpressive fellow — certainly not an obvious candidate for royal treatment. He lived a secluded existence in a tiny out-of-the-way town called Lo Debar. And because a nurse dropped him when he was five years old, Mephibosheth grew up crippled in both feet.

How surprised he must have been when the word came from Jerusalem: King David wanted to see Mephibosheth at once! No doubt he feared for his life, for in those days kings often killed any descendants of the previous king lest they make a claim to the throne. When at last Mephibosheth stood in the king's palace bowing nervously before David, he could only stammer these words: "What is your servant, that you should notice a dead dog like me?"

The king, however, was motivated by grace toward

his undeserving subject. David remembered his covenant of friendship with Jonathan, and was determined to show kindness to Jonathan's son, Mephibosheth. To everyone's surprise, David graciously granted Mephibosheth all of the land which formerly belonged to King Saul, and insisted that he eat at the king's table as a member of the royal family. The chapter ends with this touching summary: "And Mephibosheth lived in Jerusalem, because he always ate at the king's table, and he was crippled in both feet" (2 Sam 9:13).

King David's treatment of Mephibosheth illustrates the gracious way our heavenly King adopts us into His royal household. Sin has crippled and weakened us. We deserve the King's wrath, not His blessing. We may wonder, Why should the King bother to notice "dead dogs" like us? Nevertheless, God seeks us out, invites us into His presence, welcomes us at His table, and treats us like family.

Grace in the New Testament

According to the New Testament, the grace of God produces . . .

> *Goals for our lives (Acts 20:24).*
> *Gladness that we are guilt-free (Rom 8:1, 1 Tim 1:12-16).*
> *Generosity with our possessions (2 Cor 8:1-7).*
> *Gratitude for our blessings (2 Cor 9:15).*
> *Graciousness in our speech (Col 4:6).*
> *Giftedness in our service (1 Pet 4:10-11).*
> *Gentleness with others (Gal 6:1).*
> *Growth in the Lord (Titus 2:11-12, 2 Pet 3:18).*
> *Guidance in times of difficulty (2 Cor 12:7-10).*

The apostle Paul teaches that we are *saved* by grace (Rom 3:24, Titus 3:4-7), we *stand* in grace (Rom 5:2), and we *serve* by grace (Rom 12:6).

Peter speaks of "the God of all grace" who makes His people "strong, firm, and steadfast" despite our times of suffering (1 Pet 5:10).

John exclaims, "How great is the love the Father has lavished on us, that we should be called children of God! And that is what we are!" (1 John 3:1).

The writer of Hebrews reminds us, "See to it that no one misses the grace of God," and "It is good for our hearts to be strengthened by grace . . . " (Heb 12:15, 13:9).

In fact, most of the New Testament letters begin with a prayerful greeting which highlights grace: "Grace to you and peace from God our Father and the Lord Jesus Christ." In every case, the word order is the same: grace always precedes peace. This is significant because inner peace is the result of receiving God's gracious message of reconciliation. "We cannot know the peace without first receiving the grace."[6]

The grace of the Great Initiator serves as a great motivator! When Cincinnati Bengals' defensive lineman Tim Krumrie broke his leg during the first half of the 1989 Super Bowl, he refused to go immediately to the hospital. Instead, he insisted on staying in the locker room until halftime so he could speak to David Grant, the young second-string player who replaced him. Reporters and Bengals players watched as Krumrie, despite intense pain, put his enormous hands on Grant's shoulders, looked him in the eye, and urged, "Make me proud of you!" The Bengals lost the game that day, but David Grant won a lot of respect as he played the game of his life in the second half, motivated by the courageous suffering and the encouragement of his mentor.

The entire Christian life is a response to the courageous suffering and the gracious encouragement of our Master. Christ's suffering, and His resurrection victory, motivate us to do our best. If we are passionate about our work, it is because of Christ's Passionate Work on the cross. If we are driven, it is because "Christ's love compels us" (2 Cor 5:14).

God is the Great Initiator. He "began a good work in you," and intends to carry it on to completion (Phil 1:6).

GOD, THE CHEERFUL GIVER

Second Corinthians 9:7 is a great text for understanding the joy of Christian stewardship: "Each man should give what he has decided in his heart to give, not reluctantly or under compulsion, for God loves a cheerful giver." We tend to overlook, however, an important point: the reason God loves a cheerful giver is that God Himself *is* a cheerful giver! The next verse promises, "And God is able to make all grace abound to you, so that in all things at all times, having all that you need, you will abound in every good work" (2 Cor 9:8). God does not give reluctantly, grudgingly, or half-heartedly. He is a generous, cheerful, graceful giver.

He Seeks
God constantly seeks people who have wandered from His love. After Adam and Eve sinned, God came seeking for them: "But the Lord God called to the man, 'Where are you?'" (Gen 3:9).

Jesus said the Father "seeks" the kind of worshippers who honor Him "in spirit and truth" (John 4:23). The parables of the lost sheep, the lost coin, and the lost son show the Father's willingness to seek for the lost and rejoice over the found (Luke 15:1-31).[7]

During a family visit to Disney World, my daughter — just six years old at the time — was distracted as we walked through a particularly intriguing section of the park, and for a brief but terrifying moment, my wife and I thought we had lost her. Anxiously, we sought for her, and hugged her with relief when we found her standing innocently near the Dumbo ride! Any parent can comprehend the pain of losing, the intensity of searching, and the joy of finding a lost child. Amazingly, our heavenly Father comprehends it too.

He Serves

When I take my car to the garage for a tune-up, I do not expect the chairman of General Motors to serve as my mechanic. When I vacation in Washington, D. C., I do not assume the President and First Lady will wash my dirty laundry. It is laughable — no, inconceivable — that such important, powerful people would perform humble acts of service for ordinary folks.

Yet this is exactly what happened one spring evening long ago in an upper room in Jerusalem, when the King of Kings and Lord of Lords took a towel and a basin of water, stooped down, and washed His disciples' dusty feet. We rightly call Jesus "Teacher" and "Lord," but He also set a graceful example as the Cheerful Giver and the Humble Servant (John 13:1-17).

God owes us nothing; we owe Him everything. Jesus illustrated this point as follows:

> Suppose one of you had a servant plowing or looking after the sheep. Would he say to the servant when he comes in from the field, "Come along now and sit down and eat"? Would he not rather say, "Prepare my supper, get yourself ready and wait on me while I eat and drink; after that you may eat and drink"? Would he thank the servant because he did what he was told to do? So you also, when you have done everything you were told to do, should say, "We are unworthy servants; we have only done our duty" (Luke 17:7-10).

As our Master, God is not obligated to show us kindness or to thank us for faithful service. We should serve Him simply because obedience is our duty. Jesus asks,

"Who is greater, the one who is at the table or the one who serves? Is it not the one who is at the table?" Remarkably, though, Jesus goes on to say, "But I am among you as one who serves" (Luke 22:27). On another occasion, Jesus tells about an astonishing role-reversal in which the master voluntarily assumes the role of a servant:

> It will be good for those servants whose master finds them watching when he comes. I tell you the truth, *he will dress himself to serve*, will have them recline at the table and *will come and wait on them* (Luke 12:37, italics mine).

It is startling when the Master assumes a servant's role, but that is the way of grace. God reversed the expected order of things when His Son came to earth, willingly "taking the very nature of a servant" (Phil 2:7).

He Strengthens

Service makes us tired, but God offers an unending supply of strength.

> Do you not know? Have you not heard? The Lord is the everlasting God, the Creator of the ends of the earth. He will not grow tired or weary, and His understanding no one can fathom.
> He gives strength to the weary and increases the power of the weak. Even youths grow tired and weary, and young men stumble and fall; but those who hope in the Lord will renew their strength. They will soar on wings like eagles; they will run and not grow weary, they will walk and not be faint (Isa 40:28-31).

God, the Cheerful Giver, can help us find strength and joyful liberation even in simple acts of obedience. "I run in the path of your commands, for you have set my heart free" (Ps 119:32). "This is love for God: to obey His commands. And His commands are not burdensome" (1 John 5:3). In fact, while we often focus on the "commandments" God requires us to obey, the Bible also offers us several "come-and-ments" which reveal God's gracious gifts of strength to all who come to Him:

TEN "COME-AND-MENTS"

1. Come, and you will see the awesome works of God (Ps 66:5).
2. Come, and your scarlet sins will be made white as snow (Isa 1:18).
3. Come, and Christ will give you rest when you are weary and burdened (Matt 11:28).
4. Come, and Christ will make you a fisher of men (Mark 1:17).
5. Come, and your spiritual hunger and thirst will be satisfied (Isa 55:1-2, John 6:35).
6. Come, and you will never be driven away (John 6:37).
7. Come, and the Spirit will be like a stream of living water flowing from within you (John 6:37).
8. Come, and you will find mercy and grace in times of need (Heb 4:16).
9. Come, and God will come near to you (Jas 4:8).
10. Come, and you will enjoy the free gift of the water of life (Rev 22:17).

We are children of a graceful God, the Cheerful Giver.

GOD, THE ONLY SAVIOR

Six lanes wide and sixty miles long, New York's Long Island Expressway is traveled by a quarter of a million cars and trucks every day. Because of its frequent, frustrating traffic jams, commuters not-so-affectionately call this road "the world's biggest parking lot." Among New Yorkers, however, the most common name for the Long Island Expressway is simply its initials.

Every day, millions travel this wide road known as the "L.I.E."

Jesus once mentioned another wide road — a road which likewise could be called the "L.I.E.," for it represents the path of deception and falsehood. Jesus said, "Enter through the narrow gate. For wide is the gate and broad is the road that leads to destruction, and many enter through it. But small is the gate and narrow the road that leads to life, and only a few find it" (Matt 7:13-14).

Wide roads may be smooth, popular, and heavily traveled. But when faced with the choice of a spiritual pathway, Jesus warns us not to be so impressed by the number of people traveling the road that we fail to ask, "Where does this road *lead*? What is its *destination*?"

Dangers of the Wide Road

The "L.I.E.S." of Satan lead only to destruction. One subtle deception which has gained wide acceptance in recent years is the doctrine of universalism: the view that all mankind eventually will be saved. Those who hold this position emphasize God's love and grace at the expense of His wrath and righteousness. They reject the concept of Hell as a place or condition of eternal lostness. Some universalists reject the Bible entirely as an authoritative standard. Others try to show the Bible itself supports the universalist position, citing such passages as 1 Timothy 2:3-4, "God . . . wants all men to be saved and to come to a knowledge of the truth."[8]

Universalists seek for truth from all religions without affirming the superiority of any one world view. Most would agree with Origen, the third-century theologian, who believed "ultimately all would be accommodated in the majestic forgiveness and beneficence of God."[9] Perhaps without realizing it, ordinary people espouse a popular form of universalism when they say, "Oh well, we're all headed for the same place," or "Don't be so narrow-minded; Christianity is no better than any other faith," or "A loving God would never condemn anyone," or "Sincerity is all that matters." On the surface such comments seem logical but they are dangerously misleading.

The modern mood forms a particularly conducive breeding ground for universalism. From pop music artists to sports celebrities, influential persons extol the virtue of broadmindedness. A few years ago, bestselling author and lecturer Leo Buscaglia achieved national recognition with his eloquent message of self-esteem and love for one's neighbor. Unfortunately, as *Time* magazine reported:

> Buscaglia arrived at the comforting conclusion that all religions are basically alike, at least when boiled down to a readily grasped message: "All of them agree on the same principles for humanity. There is no religion that disagrees on the basic tenet being love. You can be a follower of Muhammed or Jesus or Buddha or whomever. Always they said that the most essential factor is to love your neighbor. And to love you."[10]

Such religious pluralism, according to Lesslie Newbigin, has become "the contemporary orthodoxy" and "the reigning assumption" of our culture.[11]

Graceful churches must speak plainly on this important issue. Growing gracefully does not mean embracing the popular universalism so common in our culture. In spite of its popular appeal, the view that all people will be saved contradicts the Bible in several important areas:

1. The Bible teaches the *absolute uniqueness of the true God and the salvation He offers*. God says, "I, even I, am the Lord and apart from me there is no Savior" (Isa 43:11).[12]

2. The Bible emphasizes *the absolute uniqueness and exclusive claims of Jesus Christ*. Jesus' words cannot be clearer: "I am the way and the truth and the life. No one comes to the Father except through me" (John 14:6).[13]

3. The Bible stresses *the reality of judgment, heaven, and hell*. According to Jesus, "A time is coming when all who are in their graves will hear His voice and come out — those who have done good will rise to live, and those who have done evil will rise to be condemned" (John 5:28-29).[14]

4. The Bible emphasizes *the personal responsibility of each individual in accepting God's gift of salvation*. As Moses told the Israelites, God has set before us "life and death, blessings and curses. Now choose life" (Deut 30:19).[15]

Why would the New Testament reflect such consistent urgency about evangelism if souls were not at stake? Why would Jesus say, "Make disciples of all the nations," if all were eventually to be saved anyway? Why did the apostle Paul implore people to "be reconciled to God" if such reconciliation were inevitable?

The wide road of universalism or religious pluralism will only lead the church toward apathy and uninvolvement in the vital task of evangelism.

Grace and the Narrow Road

Nevertheless, God's children must conduct ourselves gracefully even as we travel the narrow road. There are several positive responses we can make to the rising tide of relativism in our culture.

1. *We must teach the true **Biblical** universalism*. God does love the whole world! We do serve a caring God who "is patient . . . not wanting anyone to perish, but everyone to come to repentance" (2 Pet 3:9). The true universalism is not a mushy mindset, however, but a

mighty mission! The church's work continues as we gracefully tell the world the good news that Jesus saves.

2. *We must **practice** the true Biblical universalism* by demonstrating genuine compassion for all people. Racism, bigotry, cliquishness, divisiveness, and isolationism are ugly hindrances to the spread of the gospel. We must learn to be caring without being condescending, and to be judicious about obedience without being judgmental toward people. Christ does not need us to make the narrow road even narrower through rigid, legalistic, uncaring attitudes. Overcoming Satan's lies will require a heavy dose of "speaking the truth in love" (Eph 4:15).

3. *We must teach the truth.* The authority of Christ and the integrity of His Word demand that we not hesitate to proclaim "the whole will for God" (Acts 20:27), including truths which may seem unpopular or unpleasant. While we must "be merciful to those who doubt" (Jude 22), and patiently instruct those who honestly struggle with the perplexing questions of modern life, we must uphold the Biblical standard.

4. *We must gracefully disciple the nations.* If we truly believe people are lost without Christ, then love leaves us no other option. Even as we strive to find a healthy balance in our personal lives as God's servants, we must never lose the compelling motivation the apostle Paul expressed when he said, "Woe to me if I do not preach the gospel!" (1 Cor 9:16).

SUMMARY

Church growth is essentially theocentric. It all begins, and ends, with God. Both in our personal lives and in our churches, we will not get from Point A to

Point B until we know the Alpha and the Omega, the Beginner and the Finisher, the Eternal God who is the Great Initiator, the Cheerful Giver, and the Only Savior.

By grace, we are His children. He enables us to be a graceful church.

NOTES: CHAPTER SIX

[1]This quote, attributed to Simone Weil, is cited by Os Guinness in "The Cult of Relevance and the Management of Need," *Tabletalk*, June, 1992, p. 50.

[2]"Any study of Christianity (and church growth) that does not find its source, power, perspective, and focus in God will inevitably result in warped views, emphases, and conclusions. The Bible is 'fanatic' in its position on theocentricity. The Scriptures will never yield to any man-centeredness, human self-interest, or even church-centeredness." See George W. Peters, *A Theology of Church Growth* (Grand Rapids: Zondervan, 1981), p. 30.

[3]*Ibid.*, p. 97.

[4]G. Campbell Morgan described grace as follows: "Grace is first, that which delights and charms. Grace, secondly, is desire to impart to others the things that make them happy. Grace finally is the activity that does this at all costs." See G. Campbell Morgan, *Studies in the Four Gospels*, "Luke" (Old Tappan, NJ: Fleming H. Revell Company, 1931), p. 44.

[5]James Dobson, "What Wives Wish Their Husbands Knew About Women," Focus on the Family Radio Broadcast, June 1, 1992.

[6]D. Edmond Hiebert, *Titus and Philemon* (Chicago: Moody Press, 1957), p. 95.

[7]It is significant that, according to Jesus, rejoicing takes place "*in the presence of* the angels of God" when even one sinner repents (Luke 15:10, italics mine). Could it be that, in addition to the angels' own rejoicing, the Father Himself rejoices in their presence because of His own joy at the reclamation of a lost child?

[8]The most obvious, readily-identifiable proponent of this position is the Unitarian Universalist Church. Generally, the beliefs of this group include the strict humanity of Jesus; the natural rather than supernatural character of the Bible; the respect for and affirmation of a wide variety of religious beliefs and customs; and a strong sense of socio-ethical responsibility in contributing to the peace and mutual cooperation of mankind. (See Frank S. Mead, *Handbook of Denominations in the United States*, 5th edition[Nashville: Abingdon, 1970], pp. 203-206.) Typically, Jesus' virgin birth and bodily resur-

rection are rejected as unhistorical and unscientific. Members of such churches include agnostics, humanists, atheists, and nature worshipers, as well as individuals who believe in a personal God. (See Leo Rosten, ed., *Religions of America: Ferment and Faith in an Age of Crisis* [New York: Simon and Schuster, 1975], p. 267.) An ad in a community newspaper explains, "For Unitarian Universalists, you and your beliefs are the center. . . . All that is needed is a good, healthy curiosity about the world." (See *The Democrat*, Flemington, NJ: May 1, 1980.)

[9]Paul Johnson, *A History of Christianity* (New York: Atheneum, 1980), p. 111.

[10]John Leo, "The Warm Success of Dr. Hug," *Time*, November 15, 1982.

[11]Lesslie Newbigin, *The Gospel in a Pluralistic Society* (Grand Rapids: Eerdmans, 1989), p. 156.

[12]See also Deuteronomy 4:39, 6:4, 10:17; 1 Kings 8:60-61; Isaiah 33:22, 42:8, 44:6, 45:21-22; Jeremiah 3:23; Hosea 13:4; John 17:3; Romans 16:27; James 4:12; and Jude 25.

[13]See also John 8:12-24; Acts 4:12, 10:43, 16:31, 17:30-31; Philippians 2:9-11; and Revelation 22:12-16.

[14]See also Psalm 27:1-40, 96:13; Isaiah 13:11; Daniel 12:2; Matthew 10:28, 13:38-42, 13:49-50, 23:33; Mark 3:29, 16:16; John 3:36; Romans 6:23; 1 Corinthians 6:9-10; 2 Corinthians 5:10; 2 Thessalonians 1:5-9; Hebrews 9:26; and Revelation 22:17.

[15]See also Joshua 24:14-15; Ezekiel 18:20-28; and Revelation 22:17.

PART TWO:

THE GRACEFUL LEADER

7

NOBLE DESIRE: ACCEPTING THE RESPONSIBILITIES OF LEADERSHIP

Church leadership is an "unjob."

Many folks, for example, have no comprehension of what ministers do during the week. My wife and I laugh as we recall something that happened during a particularly stressful period when I found myself working eighty hours a week just to keep up. Along with preaching, teaching, and counseling, I juggled program planning, hospital visitation, late-night meetings, and other responsibilities — sacrificing precious family time to meet the needs of the church. Imagine our frustration when a middle-aged woman — a new member of the church — commented to my wife, "It must be nice to have your husband home all week!"

Our friend intended no malice with her innocent (although galling) comment. She honestly assumed that a minister basically just works on Sunday, perhaps spends a few hours "doing good" during the week, and of course invests a little extra effort during the Christmas and Easter seasons!

Calmly, but with a bit of fire in her eyes, my wife enlightened our friend about what ministers do during the week![1]

Church leadership is an "unjob" because it is seldom *understood*, often *unappreciated*, occasionally (if not frequently) *underpaid*, and subject to many *unreasonable* and *unspoken* expectations.

Further, the leader himself may see his task as an "unjob." "This isn't just a job, it's a *ministry*," he reasons

— but without some careful analysis, such thinking can eventually lead to an identity crisis for the minister, especially in mid-life.

"Jobs" come with "Job Descriptions." But whoever heard of an "*Unjob* Description?" How many hours a week does an "unjob" require? If your job is to "minister," you soon learn that the ocean of human need is too stormy for smooth sailing and too deep to bail out with your own personal bucket.

Still, the church desperately needs people who will gracefully accept the responsibilities of leadership — who find within themselves the noble desire to lead, despite their own feelings of inadequacy or the difficulty of the task. Speaking of the church's elders, for example, the Bible says, "Here is a trustworthy saying: If anyone sets his heart on being an overseer, he desires a noble task" (1 Tim 3:1). With all its difficulties, church leadership is a noble task.[2]

In healthy churches, graceful leaders tackle the "unjob" of ministry with a willing heart, not with an attitude of resentment. Mature, well-balanced leaders — who are growing gracefully in their family relationships and in their personal walk with the Lord — produce healthy churches.

It is time we gain a better *understanding* of the *unjob*. To "understand" is to better "stand under" the pressures which come with the responsibilities of leadership. It is important, therefore, to examine what leaders do, why we do it, and how God's grace supplies what is needed for the task.

ROLES OF THE CHURCH LEADER

Direction Setter

According to baseball expert Syd Thrift, a good scout

can spot a capable young player long before others recognize his potential:

> Scouting reminds me of duck-hunting. Some hunters can see the ducks way off on the horizon. Others don't see them until they come over the decoys. A few hunters don't see them until they're flying away.[3]

Like an excellent duck hunter, the church leader with vision is someone who "sees the ducks" while they are still "way off on the horizon." He wants to do more than just share in the church's work; he wants to help shape the church's dreams. Some think only about attending church next Sunday; the leader ponders what the church will be ten years from now.

True leaders set the church's direction through their faithful teaching (1 Tim 3:2, 2 Tim 2:24, Titus 1:9-14), their personal example (1 Tim 4:12, 1 Pet 5:3, Heb 13:7), and their thoughtful planning (1 Tim 5:17, Heb 13:17).

According to management expert Peter Drucker:

> Part of the leader's job is to set the spirit of the organization. That doesn't mean simply to lay out policy and plans, but to exemplify them, to pay personal attention to the areas where the vision is being worked out.[4]

Shock Absorber

"Is any one of you sick? He should call the elders of the church . . . ." (Jas 5:14).

"Brothers, if someone is caught in a sin, you who are spiritual should restore him gently" (Gal 6:1).

Churches need leaders for the same reason cars need shock absorbers. The road is not always smooth, and congregational bumps and potholes can take many forms. The leader's phone may ring with jarring news of a fatal traffic accident, a sudden illness, a family crisis, or even a community-wide emergency.

Churches need leaders for the same reason houses need lightning rods. The tension and the sparks have to come down somewhere, and they often find their outlet in church staff meetings or board meetings which deal with everything from financial problems to moral failures, from life-and-death issues to petty grievances. When critics voice their complaints, the church's leaders are usually the first to take the heat.[5]

The leader's role as shock absorber is one of those not-so-pleasant realities which ministers often learn by experience rather than by seminary training. Archibald Hart argues that church leaders should see it as a legitimate, necessary part of their role to serve as sort of a scapegoat for the group. Church leaders must be willing to face, diffuse, and properly direct expressions of anger, frustration, or criticism.[6]

There will always be bumps along the road. It is the leader's job to keep the occasional rough spots from leading to major detours.

Hope Giver

"Always be prepared to give an answer to everyone who asks you to give the reason for the hope that you have" (1 Pet 3:15). This exhortation applies to every Christian, but it applies in a special way to the church leaders, for one of the leaders' key roles is to articulate the hope of Christ both to those outside the church who ask questions about the faith, and to those inside the church who need encouragement to *continue* in the faith.

"Why have hope?" is one of the great questions of human existence. Unbelievers ask it, for they are "without hope and without God in the world" (Eph 2:12). But believers ask it too, echoing in various ways Job's anguished query, "If a man dies, will he live again?" (Job 14:14) and the desperate Ecclesiastes-like quest for meaning which asks, "Is all our labor on this earth in vain?"

In times of suffering, confusion, doubt, and death, wise leaders constantly remind their followers, "There is surely a future hope for you, and your hope will not be cut off" (Prov 23:18). Like the apostle Paul, great leaders remind those in Christ that we grieve, but "not like the rest of men who have no hope" (1 Thess 4:13), and therefore we can give ourselves "fully to the work of the Lord," knowing that "our labor in the Lord is not in vain" (1 Cor 15:58). Like Peter, great leaders remind suffering saints that God has "given us new birth into a living hope through the resurrection of Jesus Christ from the dead" (1 Pet 1:3). Great leaders urge the church to cling to the hope which serves as "an anchor for the soul, firm and secure" (Heb 6:19).

As John Dawson has pointed out, "he who gives the greatest hope gains the greatest authority."[7]

Burden Bearer

One of the trickiest balances in the church leader's tightrope walk is learning how to "carry others' burdens" (Gal 6:2) while at the same time encouraging each one to "carry his own load" (Gal 6:5). After all, the Bible says to "weep with those who weep" (Rom 12:15). Unfortunately, life contains an unending series of hurts and losses, a seemingly bottomless pit of pain, which only God Himself can handle. The Scripture does not say to "cast all your cares on your pastor," it says to cast all your cares on God (1 Pet 5:7).

Nevertheless, part of the pastoral role is burden-bearing. This can be a very weighty responsibility. It is interesting to consider the commonly-reported listing of various factors on the so-called "stress-scale." Items like marriage problems, moving to a different home, sickness, death of a close friend or relative; loss of a job and other such stressors always rank high on the list. Not only does the church leader have to deal with some of these issues as they occur in his own life, but at any given moment, he knows several people in his church who are going through these very struggles. Together, these can form an incredibly heavy burden.

In their daily work, ministers are exposed to a wide range of human hurt. They "keep watch" over God's flock as "men who must give an account" (Heb 13:17). According to F. F. Bruce, the word translated "keep watch" (Greek *agrupneo*) means they literally "lose sleep" as they vigilantly fulfill this responsibility — a fact to which weary church leaders could readily attest.[8] Even dedicated and faithful leaders eventually grow weary of feeling "responsible" all the time. As burnout approaches, some ministers experience a sense of depersonalization — a frightening sense that others are constantly *taking* from them until there is very little left to *give*.

Wise care-givers remember that the ultimate Care-Giver is God Himself. Graceful leaders recognize that the burdens are too heavy to bear alone. As the prophet foretold concerning the Messiah, "the government will be on His shoulders" (Isa 9:6). His shoulders are broad enough to carry the full weight of leadership; ours are not.

"Praise be to the Lord, to God our Savior, who daily bears our burdens" (Ps 68:19).

Team Player

Matthew's gospel lists the names of the twelve apostles in pairs (Peter and his brother Andrew, James and his brother John, Philip and Bartholomew, and so on; Matthew 10:2-4). Jesus sent them out in teams of two. When Peter preached on the day of Pentecost, he stood up "with the Eleven" (Acts 2:14), for these men stood together, united in their testimony about the resurrected Christ.[9]

Leadership is lonely work; but sometimes leaders experience unnecessary isolation and detachment. In the Old Testament, Moses nearly exhausted himself until he heeded the wise advice of his father-in-law Jethro and began sharing the load with other trusted leaders (Exod 18:13-26). Sadly, many a lonely minister has felt the emotions expressed in another Old Testament verse: "There was a man all alone . . . There was no end to his toil . . . 'For whom am I toiling, he asked, "and why am I depriving myself of enjoyment?' This too is meaningless — a miserable business!'" (Eccl 4:8). The answer, however, is found in the verses which follow:

> Two are better than one, because they have a good return for their work: If one falls down, his friend can help him up. But pity the man who falls and has no one to help him up!
> Also, if two lie down together, they will keep warm. But how can one keep warm alone? Though one may be overpowered, two can defend themselves.
> A cord of three strands is not quickly broken (Eccl 4:9-12).

In the New Testament, Paul surrounded himself with dozens of ministry partners — including a personal physician (Luke) and a dynamic prayer partner (Epaphras; see Col 4:12-14). Paul's "team" included people he called "sister," "fellow worker," "brother," and even a woman who was like a "mother" to him (Rom 16:1-24).[10] Paul's strategy for church leadership included a plurality of elders in each locale who shared the responsibilities of shepherding the flock (Acts 14:23, 20:17-35, Phil 1:1).

Graceful leaders need courage to stand alone. Nevertheless, God calls us to be team players. Pointed questions asked centuries ago by the church father, Basil of Cappadocia, compel us to avoid isolation: "How can anyone be humble, merciful, or patient, unless someone else is there? Whose feet will you wash, whom will you serve, how can you be least of all, if you are alone?"[11]

INADEQUACY OF THE CHURCH LEADER

Early in my ministry, I heard about a great preacher who urged young ministers to walk through the church during the week and pray for the people who will sit in the pews on Sunday. I have done this occasionally over the years, but even as I move quietly through the silent sanctuary, I experience a profound sense of my own inadequacy.

On Sunday, some of those pews will be filled with lively little children whose impressionable young hearts soak up the sights and sounds of church every week; I want to be a good example for them. Sunday's crowd will also include wise, mature old saints whose Bible knowledge and experience far surpass my own; still, I want to be an encouragement to these folks. As my mind continues to picture my congregation, I see dozens of teenagers and young adults who are asking tough questions about life; I see married couples struggling with the pressures of parenthood and job stress; I see dear friends struggling from the long-standing pain of loneliness, depression, sickness, and hurts of all kinds.

Although I am willing to accept the responsibility for leading these dear folks closer to God, my prayer sounds a little like Moses at the burning bush: "Who am I . . . that I should bring the Israelites out of Egypt?" (Exod 3:11). Sometimes my prayer may even resemble the anger and self-pity of Moses' angry petition offered in the wilderness:

> Why have you brought this trouble on your servant? What have I done to displease you that you put the burden of all these people on me? Did I conceive all these people? Did I give them birth? Why do you tell me to carry them in my arms, as a nurse carries an infant, to the land you promised . . . ? (Num 11:11-12).

Although I relish the task of preaching God's Word, at times I feel deeply the inadequacy of the psalmist who asked, "Who can proclaim the mighty acts of the Lord or fully declare His praise?" (Ps 106:2). As Solomon asked the Lord, "who is able to govern this great people of yours?" (2 Chr 1:10).

The apostle Paul spoke for a lot of leaders when he asked, "Who is equal to such a task?" (2 Cor 2:16).

Even though I recognize the importance of my leadership roles, I am constantly aware of the imperfect way I fulfill them. I am not always a clear-eyed direction setter; I sometimes struggle with resentment when I must repeatedly serve as the church's shock absorber; I try to give others hope, but occasionally need some encouragement myself; I am willing to be a burden bearer, but I carry some heavy burdens of my own; and even though I see myself as a team player, I still feel overwhelmed at times by my sense of personal responsibility.

Throughout my ministry, as I have helped to plant new churches and lead them toward growth, I have often felt that I was "in over my head," like David who more than once felt he was neck-deep in floodwaters (Ps 69:1-2,14-15) and at one low point in his life had to face the prophet Nathan's stinging rebuke: "You are the man!" (2 Sam 12:7). I understand the initial reluctance of Isaiah, who was called to be a prophet but saw himself as a "man of unclean lips" (Isa 6:5). I can identify with Jeremiah's hesitant disclaimer, "Ah, Sovereign Lord, I do not know how to speak; I am only a child" (Jer 1:6).

Church leadership is not just hard work — in one sense, it is *impossible* work. Karl Barth wrote:

> Can a minister be saved? I would answer that with men this is impossible, but with God all things are possible. God may pluck us as a brand out of the fire. But so far as we know, there is no one who deserves the wrath of God more abundantly than the ministers . . . Moses and Isaiah, Jeremiah and Jonah knew of a certainty why they did not want to enter into the preacher's situation. As a matter of fact, the church is really an impossibility. There can be no such thing as a minister. Who dares, who can, preach, knowing what preaching is?[12]

The leader's inadequacy finds resolution only in the grace of God. God's grace seems to be unleashed in a special way during our times of personal weakness (2 Cor 12:9). As Barth says, "We are worthy of being believed only as we are aware of our unworthiness."[13]

Moses' personal inadequacy, reflected in his question, "Who am I?" was outweighed by God's personal identity: "I am who I am" (Exod 3:14). Though David was "in over his head," he trusted God's ability to save him from the overwhelming flood (Ps 69:13). After God took away Isaiah's guilt and atoned for his sin, the prophet was free to serve with a willing heart, saying, "Here am I; send me" (Isa 6:6-8). Despite Jeremiah's youth and lack of public speaking skill, God promised to make him as strong as "a fortified city, an iron pillar and a bronze wall" (Jer 1:18). The apostle Paul recognized that we truly are not "competent to claim anything for ourselves, but our competence comes from God" who has "made us competent as ministers of a new covenant" (2 Cor 3:5-6).

MOTIVATIONS OF THE CHURCH LEADER

In premarital counseling sessions, I always ask the engaged couple, "Why are you getting married?" This seems like such a basic question, yet it must not be taken for granted. The usual answer, "Because we love one another," sometimes obscures the deeper motivations which can produce marital stress later on. Perhaps the prospective groom is motivated by a desire to escape from an unpleasant family situation at home, or perhaps the bride is hoping marriage will finally help her resolve a long-standing struggle with her own self-esteem. In any case, it is useful to probe deeper and explore the real motivations for marriage.

Similarly, it is important for church leaders to examine our motives. The question, "Why do you want to be a church leader?" is too easily answered with a response which sounds spiritual on the surface ("Because I love the Lord") but masks unhealthy motivations on the inside. In 1 Peter chapter 5, Peter addresses those who oversee the church from the perspective of a "fellow elder" (1 Pet 5:1) who understands the leadership role, and he presents three "shoulds" and three "should nots" in regard to the leaders' motivation.

First, Peter insists that leaders should serve "*not because you must, but because you are willing, as God wants you to be*" (1 Pet 5:2). Leaders must be driven by an internal impulse, not by an external compulsion. God prefers a willing heart to a twisted arm. David prayed, "Grant me a willing spirit, to sustain me" (Ps 51:12).

Second, Peter says leaders must be "*not greedy for money, but eager to serve*" (1 Pet 5:2). While it is proper for leaders to receive adequate pay (1 Cor 9:3-12, Gal 6:6, 1 Tim 5:17-18), our highest motivation must never be simply a paycheck. We cannot motivate others to place higher priority on the "treasures of heaven" if our minds are preoccupied with the "treasures of earth" (Matt 6:19-21). Many times, the rewards of Christian service cannot be deposited in a bank account or carried in a wallet. Leaders need to heed the words of Jesus: "Watch out! Be on your guard against all kinds of greed" (Luke 12:15). It diminishes our leadership role whenever we begin to think of godliness merely as "a means to financial gain" (1 Tim 6:5).

Third, Peter describes the desire of true leaders as follows: "*not lording it over those entrusted to you, but being examples to the flock*" (1 Pet 5:3). Graceful leadership points others to Christ, not to self. It exalts Christ's lordship, not the leader's personality. As the Scripture says, "There are different kinds of service, but the same Lord" (1 Cor 12:5). "For we do not preach ourselves, but Jesus Christ as Lord, and ourselves as your servants for Jesus' sake" (2 Cor 4:5).

GOD'S GRACE FOR THE CHURCH LEADER

Peter's exhortation to church leaders concludes with this word of encouragement: "And when the Chief Shepherd appears, you will receive the crown of glory that will never fade away" (1 Pet 5:4). Jesus Himself is the Chief Shepherd.[14] He is the Leader of the leaders, the Overseer of the overseers, the Shepherd of the shepherds, the King of kings. As my friends in Haiti translate this verse, Jesus is "La Grand Pastor." At Jesus' return, His faithful servants will be rewarded with an unfading crown of glory.

Resources for Ministry

God not only offers us the hope of future blessings.

He provides the resources we need now to grow grace-fully and find a healthy balance in our everyday lives. God "richly provides us with everything for our enjoy-ment" (1 Tim 6:17) and meets all our needs "according to His glorious riches in Christ Jesus" (Phil 4:19). It is helpful to notice some of the resources God graciously provides to enrich our lives as we fulfill the responsibil-ities of leadership.

1. *Physical exercise.* I neglected this area for a long time, thinking I was too busy to bother with a regular exercise program. Eventually I began to pay the price, however: lower energy levels and overall stamina, more susceptibility to colds and other minor illnesses, and an annoying feeling of tiredness most of the time. I took a closer look at Scripture, and discovered that, while the Bible emphasizes the lasting value of spiritual mat-ters, *the care of my physical health **is** a spiritual matter!* "Physical training *is of some value*" (1 Tim 4:8, italics mine). Isn't it strange how we condemn the person who harms "the temple of God" through gluttony or drunk-enness, yet praise the dedication of the stressed-out leader who abuses his body through neglect and over-work? Through maintaining a vigorous walking pro-gram over the last several years, my wife and I have discovered one of God's enjoyable resources for lasting vitality and strength.

2. *Privacy.* While preparing a Bible lesson from the gospel of Mark, I stumbled onto an interesting verse I had never considered before. Mark 7:24 says Jesus "entered a house and did not want anyone to know it." Later, the text says Jesus could not keep His presence secret, and a Syrophoenician woman came asking for His help. Nevertheless, I was impressed by the fact that Jesus sought out a place of relative privacy which offered at least a temporary respite from constant inter-action with the crowds.

Jesus often went off by Himself into the hills and found "lonely places" where He could pray without anyone else around (Mark 6:46, Luke 5:16). On one occasion, when the disciples' schedule was especially busy and stressful, He invited them, "Come with me by yourselves to a quiet place and get some rest" (Mark 6:31).

Privacy is a God-given resource for the leader who wants to grow gracefully. This means the leader will not always be available to the crowds twenty-four hours a day, seven days a week. (Since the Lord does not slumber or sleep, we can trust *Him* to be "on call" constantly.) Graceful leaders learn not to feel guilty about taking days off, scheduling time for an occasional weekend away, or taking an annual vacation away from home. Sometimes listening to the Good Shepherd's voice in private is more important than listening to the voice on the other end of a jangling telephone.

3. *Rest.* As a witty believer once noted, "Sometimes the most spiritual thing a man can do is go to bed!" It may appear noble to work unceasingly, but even God Himself rested, and designed mankind with a need for the physical and spiritual replenishing rest provides (Exod 20:8-11). "In vain you rise early and stay up late, toiling for food to eat — for He grants sleep to those He loves" (Ps 127:2). Even when Peter was arrested and chained between two soldiers in Herod's closely-guarded prison, he slept soundly and awaited the Lord's intervention (Acts 12:5ff).

Rest is a God-given resource for ministry. To neglect needed rest is to jeopardize our long-term effectiveness in Christian service and completely miss what Eugene Peterson calls "the rhythms of grace":

The Hebrew evening/morning sequence conditions us to the rhythms of grace. We go to sleep, and God begins His work. As we sleep he develops His covenant. We wake and are called out to participate in God's creative action. We respond in faith, in work. But always grace is previous and primary. We wake into a world we didn't make, into a salvation we didn't earn . . . George MacDonald once wrote that sleep is God's contrivance for giving us the help He cannot get into us when we are awake.[15]

Rewards of Ministry

Members of the church are instructed to follow their leaders obediently so that the leaders' work can be a joy, not a burden (Heb 13:17). Ultimately, this is God's intent: that we find joy, not just burdens, in our service to Christ.

Despite its difficulties, church leadership is rewarding work. We experience the joy of seeing lives changed by God's power. We share our dreams and work side by side with other people who stretch and enrich us. We constantly enjoy God's wonderful gift of *meaningfulness*, for the church leader can always know he is involved in the most important work in the world: building up the kingdom of God.

SUMMARY

Church leadership is an "unjob" unlike other tasks a person can undertake. Healthy churches need mature people who willingly accept the sometimes painful responsibilities of leadership despite their own feelings of inadequacy, and gracefully depend on God's resources.

The book of Proverbs contains this bit of wisdom for anyone who accepts the responsibility of a shepherd: "Be sure you know the condition of your flocks, give careful attention to your herds" (Prov 27:23). Along with this admonition comes a promise: once the hard work has been done "and the grass from the hills is gathered in, the lambs will provide you with clothing, and the goats with the price of a field" (Prov 27:25-26).

The message to God's leaders is both simple and reassuring: Take care of God's flock, and depend on God to take care of you.

NOTES: CHAPTER SEVEN

[1]Perhaps the only thing tougher than doing a difficult job is *doing a difficult job while others **think** you have an **easy** job!*

[2]The word "leader" certainly refers to the elders or pastors who shepherd the flock and provide spiritual oversight for the church. They are not the only ones, however, who fulfill a leadership function. Thus, the leadership principles described in this book are intended to apply more broadly to include all those whose ministry involves servant-leadership, whether one's specific role means serving as a preacher, teacher, deacon, youth director, small group leader, or some other position of responsibility within the church.

[3]Syd Thrift in *The Game According to Syd*, cited by John Erardi in *The Cincinnati Enquirer*, February 28, 1993.

[4]Peter Drucker, "Managing to Minister," *Leadership*, Spring, 1989, p. 20.

[5]When King Herod decided to persecute the church, he began by killing one prominent leader (James) and by arresting another (Peter; see Acts 12:1-2).

[6]Archibald Hart, Lecture on "The Minister and Anger," Fuller Theological Seminary, April 30, 1992.

[7]John Dawson, *Taking Our Cities for God* (Lake Mary, FL: Creation House, 1989), pp. 42-43.

[8]F.F. Bruce, *The Epistle to the Hebrews* (Grand Rapids: Eerdmans, 1964), pp. 407-408.

[9]George W. Peters, *A Theology of Church Growth* (Grand Rapids: Zondervan, 1981), p. 125.

[10]The team ministry concept is presented as a church-planting model by David W. Shenk and Ervin R. Stutzman in *Creating Communities of the Kingdom* (Scottdale, PA: Herald Press, 1988), pp. 42-55.

[11]Cited by Shenk and Stutzman, *Ibid.*, p. 45.

[12]Karl Barth, *The Word of God and the Word of Man*, translated by Douglas Horton (Grand Rapids: Zondervan, 1935), p. 126.

[13]*Ibid.*, p. 129.

[14]The Greek word *archipoimenos* ("chief shepherd") appears only here in the New Testament.

[15]Eugene Peterson, "The Pastors' Sabbath," *Leadership*, Spring, 1985, pp. 53-54.

8

GIVE YOUR HOUSEHOLD A HAND: GRACE FOR THE LEADER'S FAMILY

When my wife and I lead workshops on marriage enrichment, sometimes we begin by giving couples a short piece of rope and asking them to do something with the rope to symbolize their homelife. For example, one couple frayed the ends of the rope to illustrate the tension in their home. Another couple simply pulled the rope from both ends, demonstrating the tug-of-war in which they sometimes engage. Others pulled the rope into a loop open at one end, to show how their family circle opens up to others with the love of God. Much to his wife's chagrin, one humorist in the group tied his rope in a hangman's noose!

Probably the most encouraging response is when the couple simply ties the rope into a firm knot. God says, when a couple marries "the two become one flesh" (Gen 2:24). Families offer needed companionship — God's solution to the problem of loneliness. They provide a basis for moral instruction and discipleship — a place where love for God and His Word can be discussed "when you sit at home and when you walk along the road, when you lie down and when you get up" (Deut 6:4-7).[1] Jesus affirmed the value of family ties when He said, "Therefore what God has joined together, let man not separate" (Matt 19:4-6). Oddly, though, many active Christians find that their busy involvement in church work sometimes threatens to pull their families apart instead of tying them closer together.

Some of life's toughest tests take place at home, for

in a real sense, the family serves as the proving ground for authentic leadership. The Bible says, "Love your neighbor," and our closest neighbors are those who live under our own roof. If we struggle with impatience, anger, worry, or selfishness, these weaknesses will show at home. Those who live with us on a daily basis know whether or not we really are graceful people. The question of 1 Timothy 3:5 looms large for all who lead: "If anyone does not know how to manage his own family, how can he take care of God's church?"

Effective ministry to one's own family is one of the most important issues in a minister's personal life. Yet this becomes extremely difficult when a growing church demands increasing amounts of the leader's time and energy. According to a survey of 748 ministers, 94 percent said they feel pressure to have "an ideal family," yet 81 percent said they have "insufficient time together" with their spouse.[2]

To become graceful leaders, we must learn to be graceful at *home*. How can we devote ourselves to church growth without slighting the needs of our spouses and children? How can we "give our households a hand"? What does it mean for a *family* to "grow gracefully"?

THE TIES THAT BIND

Treasuring the Family

Mary's experience was unique as she gave birth to Jesus and then watched Him grow up. Yet every parent can identify with the way she "treasured up all these things and pondered them in her heart" (Luke 2:19, 2:51). The heart is a treasure chest, and family memories are some of the most precious gems stored there.

I treasure my own boyhood memories which impacted my life. Our church used to provide little cardboard boxes of offering envelopes which contained one envelope for each Sunday of the year. When I was about six years old, my dad hammered three little tacks into the door frame of our family room, and he solemnly instructed my two brothers and me to hang our offering boxes on the tacks. Each week, I took out my envelope and put a nickel inside for the church offering.

A couple of years ago, the old house where I grew up needed to be torn down to make room for construction of a new house. My dad and I went into the old house to salvage a few items, and I happened to walk over to the old door frame. After more than thirty years, those three tacks were still there. I pulled them out with my hammer, and keep them now on my dresser as a reminder of the treasured influence a dad can have on his son. My dad not only drove some tacks in the wall that day long ago; he tacked an important lesson onto my heart — a lesson about priorities, stewardship, and consistent love for God.

My wife and I treasure memories of our courtship and marriage: our first date, our first kiss, our first apartment. Our wedding day, August 31, 1975, was a day of so much joy we smiled until our faces hurt! We treasure the days when our older two children were born, and the day when our youngest child was adopted. We treasure memories of first teeth, first haircuts, and first days of school; priceless child-painted artwork displayed on the refrigerator with magnets; wrestling matches on the family room floor; the vacation when we were drenched by a sudden storm at the Grand Canyon.

By His grace, God has given us much to treasure in our families. It is good to ponder these things in our hearts.

Tears for the Family

Nevertheless, families can also produce some of our heaviest burdens and deepest hurts. Families are not only something to treasure; they are also a source of tears. Even while Jesus was just a tiny baby, Mary heard Simeon's solemn prediction that her child would be "a sign that will be spoken against," and "*a sword will pierce your own soul too*" (Luke 2:33-35, italics mine). Mary's child was the unique Son of God; yet every parent faces times when "swords pierce our souls" because of painful events in the lives of our children.[3]

The Bible is utterly realistic about the tears leaders face within their own homes, presenting a virtual encyclopedia of family problems:

Violence in the home of Adam: Cain killed his brother Abel (Gen 4:1-16).

Favoritism in the homes of Isaac and Jacob: bitter rivalries among their children were the result (Gen 25:19-27:41, 37:1-36).

Sexual unfaithfulness and internal strife in the home of David: David committed adultery with Bathsheba, Amnon raped his sister Tamar, Absalom and Adonijah led rebellions against their father's authority (2 Sam 11:1-27, 13:1-38, 15:1-18:33, 1 Kgs 1:1-53).

The Bible describes family problems of all kinds, from childlessness to childish rebellion, from widowhood to emotional cruelty.

God understands the heartaches families experience. But even our hurts can be opportunities for His grace to work in our lives. Shared tears can tie a family closer together. As the word "hospitality" suggests, our homes can be "hospitals" where hurting people are nursed back to health by the tenderness of God's grace.

Time for the Family

A wise friend once told me, "LOVE is spelled T-I-M-E." Time together is indispensable. If we are searching for "ties that bind," we must be willing to spend the "*time* that binds" our families together.

Time is a precious, nonrenewable resource. The growing-up years of our children quickly pass and are difficult to reclaim if we do not make the most of the opportunities they afford. Yet time pressure is one of the greatest demands of leadership, and the balance of family time with public ministry creates an ongoing tension.

One day, when my wife, Candy, expressed some frustration with my busy schedule, I challenged her to write down some specific changes she wished we would make. Here is what she wrote:

WHAT I WISH OUR LIFE COULD BE

1. I wish we were less pressured, especially on weekends.
2. I wish we could have more relaxed evenings, more time to go out on "dates," more fun and less responsibility.
3. I wish we weren't always too tired to have people over to our home simply to socialize and form stronger friendships.
4. I wish we felt less pressure to "grow a church," and we could just be "ordinary people" for awhile.

HOW WE COULD ACHIEVE THESE GOALS

1. Learn to say "no" more often without feeling guilty or worrying what others will think.
2. Make "dates" or special nights out more of a priority.
3. Once in awhile, don't attend church functions where our presence is not absolutely necessary, or occasionally attend a different church where we can just "sit."
4. Get away more often; take short weekend trips just for fun.
5. Change our work-oriented mindset to allow more room for being ourselves and enjoying life.

I am grateful for my wife's wisdom. I am also grateful she did not write a longer list!

Time management which "gives our household a hand" is a difficult but necessary skill for graceful leaders. The Bible tells husbands to love our wives as Christ loved the church, not to love the church at the expense of our wives.

COUPLES IN MINISTRY

The Bible contains a surprising amount of information about couples in ministry (see Appendix Three, page 215). Both singleness and marriage bring certain advantages and disadvantages to ministry (1 Cor 7:32-35, 9:5), but for the married leader, there are a number of areas in which growing gracefully is required.

Realities of Married Life

Like all married couples, church leaders and our spouses can expect to encounter various phases in our relationships.

First, there are the *"wows,"* those exciting initial stages of courtship when we first discover our mutual attraction and interest in each other. Though the honeymoon eventually ends, and our initial infatuation eventually gives way to a deeper kind of love, every marriage needs a "wow" now and then. Romance, fun, and spontaneity need never die. I am determined never to be a "stalemate" and allow my relationship with my mate to grow stale and dull. A married man should never forget the proverb's advice: "rejoice in the wife of your youth" (Prov 5:18).

Along with the "wows" come the *"vows,"* those solemn promises of loyalty and commitment made on the wedding day. Years ago, I heard about a couple who got married while standing on the Rock of Gibraltar. Wherever our weddings take place, Christian marriages are grounded on the solid rock of Christ and His Word. His strength and grace undergird our lives together. Unfaithfulness to the marriage vows cripples a person's prayers and spiritual leadership (1 Pet 3:7). "So guard yourself in your spirit, and do not break faith with the wife of your youth" (Mal 2:15).

Most of married life, however, simply consists of the "*nows*," the day-to-day realities of life together. In healthy marriages, couples find joy in the "ordinaries" of simple blessings like breaking daily bread and sharing a nightly bed. Along with mutual respect and trust, one of the most important ingredients of a lasting marriage is simply the ability to be content with each other. The unhealthy drivenness which often characterizes success-oriented people tends to weaken our capacity for contentment.

"Better a dry crust with peace and quiet than a house full of feasting with strife" (Prov 17:1). Graceful leaders learn to be "content whatever the circumstances" during the "nows" of daily living (Phil 4:11).

PAIN in a Leader's Marriage

Four particularly vexing problems threaten the well-being of a church leader's marriage. We can identify them by using the acrostic PAIN, which stands for Priorities, Anger, Identity, and Neglect.

Priorities are always difficult, since the leader has to balance church work with family needs. Caring for one's family is not a *departure* from ministry; in a real sense, it *is* ministry. It is "seeking first the kingdom of God" by allowing God to reign supreme in our own households. As one minister's wife wrote:

I don't resent the priority my husband places on his

ministry. I've always appreciated feeling, though, that Gary's time is as available to me as it is to the congregation.

Even though he's often called away by emergencies over which he has no control, he's consistently communicated to me that I'm his first choice, that he would rather be home with me than running off to tend a crisis or attend a meeting.[4]

Anger is another part of the leader's pain. Frustration with church people and church problems can spill over into our marriages. At one point in our marriage, Candy and I noticed that our daily communication with each other began to consist mainly of negative, angry discussions of church-related issues. We even managed to ruin more than one evening out at a restaurant by allowing church problems to dominate the conversation from salad to dessert. "'In your anger do not sin': Do not let the sun go down while you are still angry" (Eph 4:26). This is good advice for anyone, but leadership couples should give it special consideration.

Identity is another struggle for couples in ministry. Many church leaders make the mistake of defining our selves by what we do. Trying to "be all things to all people," we lose sight of who we really are. This problem is compounded if the minister's spouse is unsure of her own identity. Many times, the spouse of a minister has to deal with role expectations which make it difficult for her just to be herself.

As Bill and Lynne Hybels explain:

Some people get lost along the way because they have low self-esteem. Others end up with low self-esteem because they got lost along the way. For years they treat others as if they are more important than themselves, and eventually they begin to believe it.[5]

Sadly, when one spouse loses his or her identity, the

other ends up "loving a mirage," and the truth is "you can't hug air."[6]

Ruth Senter describes the dilemma in her book, *The Guilt-Free Book for Pastor's Wives*:

> I have the feeling that many times we don't get around to being loving, kind, gentle, patient, peaceful, confident, honest, etc., because we are too busy worrying about what we should do. Thus, activity, rather than character, becomes the gauge for our spirituality, and outward performances become more important than inward conditions . . .
>
> . . . the Christian life is not performing; it is being. It is not filling a role or playing a part, but responding to life offstage and out of the glare of the lights.
>
> . . . God isn't out to stuff us into a mold that doesn't fit. He doesn't expect us to counterfeit resources because of whose wife we happen to be or because of what we think others are expecting from us.[7]

According to Karen Norheim, the identity problem can be overcome only if we *maintain the right attitude* (serving to the glory of God), *cultivate constant gratitude* (giving thanks for the positive things God is doing in our lives), and *give others lots of latitude* (expressing God's grace by responding to others with mercy and acceptance).[8]

Neglect is one of the most painful threats to a leader's marriage. The busy lifestyle and heavy responsibilities of leadership can lead to neglect of one's spouse, children, or self, not to mention one's own personal relationship with the Lord.

As Bill Hybels notes, busy people tend to fall into a crisis mode which causes us to neglect in-depth personal relationships.

> Crisis mode living is when you spend every waking moment of every day trying to figure out how to keep all your balls in the air and all your plates spinning. In cri-

sis mode you keep running faster and faster, from project to project, deadline to deadline, quota to quota,
meeting to meeting, sermon to sermon. Your RPMs keep
creeping higher and higher until you hit the red line.

Most active people have to spend a certain amount of
time in crisis mode. Life just turns out that way. . . .

The problem arises when you spend too much time in
crisis mode. That's when crisis mode goes from being a
season of life to becoming a way of life.[9]

The result is what Hybels calls "skimming," sliding
along on the surface, shortchanging our investment of
energy in important relationships. We become superficial with our spouse, children, and friends — even in
our walk with God — eventually depleting our emotional resources.[10]

Oddly, if you asked most Christian leaders what is
most important to them, their answer would certainly
include their families; yet our daily schedules often tell
a different story — a story of pain and even neglect of
the priceless people God graciously has placed in our
homes.

The Graceful Spouse

"By wisdom a house is built, and through understanding it is established; through knowledge its rooms
are filled with rare and beautiful treasures" (Prov 24:3-
4).

Graceful marriages are built with *understanding on
the inside.* "Husbands, . . . be considerate as you live
with your wives" (1 Pet 3:7). If our public ministry
requires the empathy of a good listener and the sensitivity of a thoughtful counselor, we may be tempted to
turn off these skills when we go home. However, as
Jorie Gulbranson points out:

Bringing home those counseling skills — being a good
listener and empathizer — is as important in your home

as it is at church — perhaps more important.

Unless those skills are available at home, a pastor's wife can easily resent those who have access to her husband. If pastors can listen intently, looking in the eyes of their parishioners, showing care and compassion, their wives deserve the same treatment at home.[11]

Extra understanding is required because of the special demands leadership places upon the marriage.[12] We must remember we are married to our spouse, not to the church. We must empower our spouses with the freedom to decide what avenues of Christian service are right for them instead of compelling them to fit a stereotypical mold.

Graceful marriages are built with *support from the outside*. Church programming must not be allowed to crowd out adequate time for family togetherness. Ministry couples need to protect their own "alone time" and network with other couples who can provide mutual encouragement as well as child-care "trades" to save on babysitting costs. Leadership retreats can be planned to include both husbands and wives. In graceful churches, sermons and Bible classes must address the need to live a balanced life and encourage the concept that serving the Lord includes ministry to our own families.

Most important, graceful marriages are built with *strength from the Lord*. We cannot do it on our own; but with the help of God, we can avoid reaching a "stalemate." We can find lasting joy as a married couple who also happen to be a ministry couple.

STRUGGLES OF A CRADLE CHRISTIAN

I was born on a Friday morning in 1954. The following Sunday, my parents took me to church.

Our church building was already a century old then, and my brothers and I were the fourth generation of my family to attend. If not the backbone of the church, we at least qualified as a vertebra or two! My great-grandfather had read Scripture from the carved oak pulpit that still graced the platform.

Over the years, my brothers and I progressed through the optimistically named Helping Hands preschool class to the Loyal Sons and Daughters class for teens. In the process, without trying very hard, we memorized Scripture texts like John 3:16 and hymns like "Amazing Grace." We absorbed a smorgasbord of spiritual sensations: the sound of a clanging church bell and a ticking antique wall clock, the smell of Communion juice, the feel of oak pews and crumpled take-home papers.

While many people my age consider themselves Baby Boomers or Yuppies, I am better characterized as a Cradle Christian or a BUICK (a Brought Up In Church Kid). Most churches contain people like me who have been taught about the Lord since birth. When we read Paul's words to Timothy to remember "how from infancy you have known the holy Scriptures" (2 Tim 3:15), we can identify.

And without hesitation, we can list the advantages of a Christian childhood. Like many other Cradle Christians, I was blessed with parents who stayed together, who taught me right from wrong, who prayed and held hands around the dinner table, who respected the authority of God's Word, who tithed even during lean times, who consistently modeled godly values and taught me the way of salvation. Today, as the father of three, I am doing all I can to bring up my own children in the nurture and admonition of the Lord.

Nevertheless, despite the blessings of my Christian upbringing, I am convinced that Cradle Christians face unique struggles that are often misunderstood or simply overlooked. These problems are magnified when children grow up in a church *leader's* home. How can our *children* grow gracefully?

Identifying the Struggles

The Doubting Dilemma. Cradle Christians commonly experience a time of intense questioning, not only during adolescence, but even into adulthood. "Is my faith really my own, or is it merely a reflection of my upbringing? What do I really believe about the Bible, about prayer, about the church?"

Worship Burnout. By the time Cradle Christians graduate from high school, they have sat through hundreds of worship services, Bible classes, youth group sessions, and other church-related meetings. Spiritual dullness can grow as familiar hymns seem *too* familiar, public prayers seem too predictable, and worship routines seem more habitual than heartfelt. Cradle Christians long to rekindle the joyous intensity of the psalmist who exclaimed, "I rejoiced with those who said to me, 'Let us go to the house of the Lord'" (Ps 122:1).

Shattered Idealism. Growing up in the church, one sees firsthand the imperfection and inconsistency of God's people. Up close, the honest observer can find plenty of spots, stains and wrinkles on the bride of Christ. Childish idealism melts into disillusionment when, moments after the end of a sermon about the love of God, one hears a slanderous piece of gossip on the front steps of the church building. Church rhetoric says we exist to glorify God. Church reality says we battle over budgets and nitpick over picnics. Cradle Christians see the church up close and personal. Sometimes it is not pretty.

Top That Testimony. Fellow believers unwittingly add to a Cradle Christian's discomfort through testimonial one-up-manship. My life story sounds bland compared to the exciting experiences of friends who turned to Christ from drug abuse or other paths of desperation. Unlike the prodigal son, Cradle Christians are more like the prodigal's older brother, who labored faithfully for his father, never straying far from home.

Self-Righteousness. When I was growing up, my parents taught me to "be good." But being "good" isn't good enough! Remember the rich young ruler? When Jesus reminded him about the commandments, the young man boldly declared, "Teacher, all these I have kept since I was a boy" (Mark 10:20). This fellow seemed to have it all: money (he was rich), health (he was young), power (he was a ruler), and decency (he was a "good" man). But as the conversation continued, Jesus showed that, in spite of appearances, the fellow's priorities were wrong: his love for wealth prevented a full commitment to Christ.

Others may not see obvious sins in their lives, but in the battleground of the heart, Cradle Christians fight the tempter daily. The subtle hazard of spiritual smugness must be overcome.

Help for the Struggler

What can believing parents do about these problems as we bring up the next generation of Cradle Christians? And how can grown-up Cradle Christians deal with our personal struggles? Here are some suggestions.

Suggestions for Parents

1. Communicate. Prepare your children for the struggles they will encounter, especially as they approach adolescence. Discuss current issues in light of scripture. Talk frankly about doubts. Avoid being shocked or defensive when questions arise. Jude 22 wisely counsels, "Be merciful to those who doubt."

2. Establish Contact with Non-Christians. Do not isolate your family from the unchurched. Faith grows through interacting with others, sharing their struggles, hearing their questions, and understanding their hurts. Get involved with community events, sports, or neighborhood volunteer work. Cultivate the habit of inviting non-Christian neighbors over for dinner.

3. Battle Spiritual Boredom. Since God is truly alive today, irrelevance is a form of irreverence! Explore creative methods for family devotions. My wife and I encourage our children to take turns leading our supper time prayers. My son enjoys writing short stories, and our girls like to think of choruses to sing. One summer, our family made it a goal to read the Gospel of John and informally discuss a chapter or two each week while sitting on the porch swing or driving in the car. By participating in short-term mission trips and by helping with our church's local outreach efforts, my family has found freedom to serve Christ in fresh new ways.

4. Strive for Authenticity. Not only should we "fight the good fight of faith," parents also need to fight the good fight of *fake!* Children sense — and rebel against — any kind of phoniness. Parents must model a genuine, healthy self-image as forgiven children of God. The apostle Paul presented the right balance when he said, "By the grace of God I am what I am" (1 Cor 15:10). "By the grace of God" speaks of humble self-denial; "I am what I am" speaks of sincere self-acceptance. Children reared in Christian homes desperately need to find this balance.

Suggestions for the Cradle Christian

1. Accept Responsibility for Personal Growth. No matter what our childhood was like, there comes a time when we must let go of the past, both good and bad, and press on.

"When I became a man, I put childish ways behind me," wrote the apostle Paul (1 Cor 13:11). He could have been proud of his past, for he was brought up in a strict, law-abiding Jewish home. Or he could have been ashamed of his past, for he persecuted the church and was "the worst of sinners" (1 Tim 1:16). But instead, Paul was determined to forget what was behind (both his successes and his sins) and press on toward the goal (Phil 3:4-14).

Cradle Christians, like other believers, need to follow the twofold prescription for maturity found in 2 Peter 3:18: "grow in the grace and knowledge of our Lord and Savior Jesus Christ."

Grow in grace. Jesus said, "He who has been forgiven little loves little" (Luke 7:47). Our love for God increases as we recognize His forgiveness. Although I was brought up in a godly environment, it was still "amazing grace that saved a wretch like me."

Grow in knowledge. In my case, the questioning during my teenage years drove me to study why I believe. Thanks to the patience of my parents and the guidance of youth leaders at church, I found answers to satisfy my mind.

2. Turn Frustrations into Fruit. Properly channeled, dissatisfaction with the status quo can be *good*. If Cradle Christians feel bored and restless in church, let them respond with positive correction, not negative rejection.

Tom, for example, was brought up in the church and sat through many worship services over the years, some dull, some delightful. He learned from his experiences, and today Tom serves as a worship leader in a thriving church where he helps plan worship experiences filled with variety and inspiration.

3. Be Grateful. Despite the struggles, I am thankful to be a Cradle Christian.

I am grateful for the privilege of serving God longer! Like Timothy, I had a head start because of my early training, and I was able to begin serving the Lord as a young man. Many people who come to Christ later in life wish they had enjoyed such an opportunity.

I am grateful for parents who prayed for me before I was born and taught me about God's love even before I could understand. I want to be that kind of parent myself.

SUMMARY

When Theodore Roosevelt visited the Grand Canyon, he said, "Do nothing to mar its grandeur, for the ages have been at work upon it and man cannot improve it. Keep it for your children, your children's children, and all who come after you."[13]

Similarly, God has given a grand and lasting gift to the world in His plan for the Christian family. "The promise is for you and your children and for all who are far off" (Acts 2:39). Even as we strive to lead the church toward growth, let us do nothing to mar the grandeur of the home. Instead, let us strengthen the ties that bind our hearts in Christian love.

Our spouses need us. Our children need us. It is time for church leaders to give our households a hand.

NOTES: CHAPTER EIGHT

[1]It is instructive to note how, according to the New Testament, whole households sometimes accepted Christ and were baptized (Acts 16:15, 16:31-34, 18:8, 1 Cor 1:16). From infancy, Timothy had learned the Scripture from his godly mother and grandmother (2 Tim 1:5, 3:15).

[2]David Goetz, "Is the Pastor's Family Safe at Home?" *Leadership*, Fall, 1992, p. 39.

[3]Mary's hardships were many. Soon after Jesus was born, she and Joseph had to travel to Egypt to escape from King Herod's wrath (Matt 2:13-23). Later, the people in her hometown of Nazareth refused to accept Jesus, and He did not even perform many miracles there because of their unbelief (Matt 13:53-58, Luke 4:16-30). Mary's other sons did not believe in Jesus at first (John 7:3-5), and at one point, she and her sons tried to take charge of Jesus, fearing He was out of His mind (Mark 3:20-21). Her greatest pain, no doubt, occurred when she stood on Calvary's hill and watched her blessed Son died by crucifixion (John 19:25-27).

[4]Jorie Gulbranson, "What Every Pastor's Wife Wants from Her Husband," *Leadership*, Fall, 1992, p. 24.

[5]Bill and Lynne Hybels, *Fit to Be Tied* (Grand Rapids: Zondervan, 1991), pp. 203-204.

[6]*Ibid.*, p. 205.

[7]Ruth Senter, *The Guilt-Free Book for Pastor's Wives* (Wheaton, IL: Victor Books, 1990), pp. 14-17.

[8]Karen Norheim, *Mrs. Preacher: Succeeding as a Minister's Wife* (Joplin: College Press, 1985), p. 39.

[9]Bill and Lynne Hybels, *Fit to Be Tied*, pp. 177-178.

[10]*Ibid.*, pp. 178-179.

[11]Jorie Gulbranson, "What Every Pastor's Wife Wants," p. 25.

[12]Nathan Brown points out that the typical minister's wife faces just as much interpersonal stress as her husband does, but because of her role, she often has less power to do anything about the problems. This places her in a position of significant vulnerability (Nathan Brown, Lecture on "Social Networks and Burnout," Fuller Theological Seminary, April 29, 1992).

[13]"The Guide," published by Grand Canyon National Park (Volume XV, Number 6, June 28-August 22, 1992), p. 11.

9
METEORIZED MINISTERS: GRACE TO HANDLE WORRY

As part of a church planting team, my job was to find an adequate meeting place for our newly-formed congregation to rent. Still unsuccessful after weeks of legwork, I was feeling discouraged. Our target date for starting the church was approaching rapidly, and we had exhausted most of our options. The shadows seemed long and grim as I returned home on a late autumn afternoon and trudged into my bedroom with feet dragging and spirit sagging.

Then I saw the note. Carefully placed on top of my dresser, neatly printed in Number Two pencil lead, it contained a message from my then nine-year-old daughter:

Dear Daddy,
  You may be discouraged, but I'm sure that if you are trying to teach people about the word of God, He won't let you down. So don't worry! Everything is going to be fine!

With love,
Michelle.

Later, I thanked Michelle for her encouraging words, but inwardly I chuckled at her naivete. "If only it were really that easy," I thought.

But to my amazement, just two days later, we found an ideal meeting place for the church: a community center with large clean rooms, adequate parking, and reasonable rent. Grateful, yet a little embarrassed at my lack of faith, I posted my daughter's note on the bulletin board above my desk and sat pondering her simple wisdom: "Don't worry, Daddy."

Jesus knew His followers would struggle with worry. When He urged His disciples, "Do not set your heart on what you will eat or drink; do not worry about it" (Luke 12:29), the word translated "worry" is *meteorizomai*, an interesting term used only once in the New Testament.

Ancient astronomers observed that shooting stars appeared neither in outer space nor in the earth's inner atmosphere. They were "meteors," objects of midair. Likewise, *meteorizomai* figuratively describes the way worry leaves a person hanging in midair. Worried people are "hung up," caught in the middle, suspended in space instead of planted solidly on the ground.[1]

ARMY OF THE ANXIOUS

I hate to admit it, but at times I am a meteorized minister. And I am not alone. Worry is a common pastoral pitfall, a sin which easily entangles church leaders. We attend seminars on time management and money management, but deep inside we realize the real battle has to do with mind management.

We long to be, in the words of G. Campbell Morgan, "free from fret and friction and feverishness."[2] But beneath the friendly smiles and wise words, despite the genuine joy we experience in serving God, we are all meteorized ministers at times. We are the fraternity of the fretful, the army of the anxious, the brotherhood of the bothered.

Even great heroes of the faith struggled with worry. Paul wrote, "Do not be anxious (Greek *merimnao*) about anything" (Phil 4:6), yet he also admitted that he wrestled with this problem every day as he faced the daily

154

pressure of his "concern (*merimna*) for all the churches" (2 Cor 11:28). Martha confessed beautiful words of confidence in Jesus (John 11:21-27), but the stress of household preparations made her "worried and upset about many things" (Luke 10:38-42).

Church leaders face a difficult dilemma. We walk a tightrope between legitimate concern and sinful worry, between pleasing the Good Shepherd and pleasing the sheep, between casting our cares on the Lord and accepting the proper responsibilities and pressures of ministry.

How can we demonstrate compassion for our people and their problems without taking upon ourselves a crushing load of emotional stress? When does our intense concern for the church's well-being cross the line and become a sinful kind of worry? We need God's grace to find the balance.

UNDERSTANDING THE REAL PROBLEM

To clarify the issue, I have made a list of items which worry does *not* include.

What Worry Is Not

Burden-bearing is not worry. Members of the body need to share the load of emotional pain (1 Cor 12:26). Romans 12:15 says to "mourn with those who mourn." When I carry a burden of concern for my brothers, I am not worrying; I am fulfilling the law of Christ (Gal 6:2).

Nervous tension is not worry. I have learned to accept the pressure which builds each week as I work on Sunday's sermon, and the little rush of apprehension about Thursday's board meeting, as healthy stimuli which the Holy Spirit uses to spur me toward greater zeal and productivity.

Attention to detail is not worry. I want the custodian to keep the church lawn neatly mowed and trimmed, not because I am a worrier, but because our church property should reflect a valid concern for excellence.

Planning is not worry. Thoughtful planning actually reduces worry. I keep in my briefcase a folder labeled "Plans." When tempted to fret about church problems, I try instead to jot down practical steps for problem-solving or ideas which will help carry out our church's goals.

Weariness is not worry. Most of us can identify with the words of comedian Flip Wilson, who said, "If I had my entire life to live over, I doubt if I'd have the strength."[3] After Elijah's contest with the prophets of Baal, he sprawled under a tree, exhausted and hungry. He needed (and God provided) food, drink and rest before returning to service (1 Kgs 19:1-9). I am learning to discern the difference between feeling worried and feeling wearied.

Sorrow is not worry. Jesus was never guilty of sinful worry, yet He was sorrowful and troubled in Gethsemane (Matt 26:37,38). He insisted that His followers take up their cross daily, which includes a willingness to assume the risk of emotional pain. Hurts come with ministry. Christian leaders should not be surprised when painful trials come (1 Pet 4:12).

What Worry Is

Nevertheless, we need to recognize the symptoms which indicate that our godly concern has crossed the line into sinful worry.

Sinful worry means *worldliness*: preoccupation with items like clothes and food (Matt 6:25). Jesus warned that "the worries of this life, the deceitfulness of wealth and the desires for other things" are thorns which choke the word and make it unfruitful (Mark 4:18, 19).

Sinful worry means *wastefulness*. Instead of adding hours to life (Matt 6:27), worry leads to hours of lost productivity as ministers stare blankly at their office walls, stewing over unresolvable problems. Some preachers even waste precious hours of their long-awaited vacation, worrying about the church crises which surely await them when they return home!

And perhaps its most devastating characteristic: sinful worry means *weakness*. Our word "worry" comes from the Old English *wyrgan*, to strangle. Worry strangles vision, chokes creativity, weakens passion. Stripped of vigor, the worried minister wastes time in September, dreading the church's annual meeting which will occur in November.

Worry prevents him from preaching boldly and acting decisively. As Henry Ward Beecher said, "Worry is rust upon the blade."[4] Suffering the paralysis of analysis, the worried minister magnifies small troubles into unfounded, even irrational fears, like the proverbial wicked man who "flees though no one pursues" (Prov 28:1). Archibald Hart insists, "Worry and joy *cannot* coexist. Worry extinguishes joy."[5]

HUMBLE HINTS FOR THE WORRIER

Since most of us must fight a lifelong battle with anxiety, I humbly offer the following observations:

Prayer is vital. "Cast all your anxiety on him because he cares for you" (1 Pet 5:7). Prayer is not just spiritual escapism. It is God's divinely-appointed alternative to anxiety (Phil 4:6). It leads to stronger confrontation of problems, greater contentment in ministry, and deeper confidence in God. Jesus often prayed, but He never pouted.

Recently I read a newspaper article which suggested

that the way to overcome worry is to set aside a half-hour every day for your own personal fretting time, in a private place where you will not be interrupted. Another news item told how entrepreneurs are opening "Serenity Salons" where stressed-out clients can spend an hour relaxing on a comfortable couch surrounded by gentle music and videotaped mountain scenery — all for a stiff fee. Devotions in the prayer closet provide a more Scriptural alternative.

Maturity helps. "A wise man has great power, and a man of knowledge increases strength" (Prov 24:5). As time passes and experience grows, it becomes a little easier to accept oneself and the pressures of ministry. Youthful ministers are especially vulnerable to the common but foolish error of trying to please everyone. Anxiety multiplies as congregational whims jostle the young leader.

Carl Sandburg provided a useful illustration when he told of the chameleon, famous for its ability to conform to any surroundings, which died while trying to move across two or three yards of Scotch plaid![6] Age and experience bring the wisdom to avoid such self-destruction.

Friends help. "As iron sharpens iron, so one man sharpens another" (Prov 27:17). Encouraging friends provide a release valve for built-up tensions, and healing humor when we take ourselves too seriously. Trustworthy friends who "spur one another on toward love and good deeds" (Heb 10:24) offer top-quality anxiety relief.

GROUP GRACE: OVERCOMING
THE LONE RANGER SYNDROME

Shortly before sunrise on a quiet Wednesday morning, a dozen sleepy saints gathered in our church building to pray.

A few weeks before, when I announced the beginning of this early morning prayer service, I wondered who would come. But now I smiled as this diverse little flock pulled their folding chairs into a circle.

Jim, our church custodian clad in his work clothes, settled into his seat next to Richie, an accountant dressed in suit and tie. Seventeen-year-old Mike, a zealous new Christian, hurried into the room for a few minutes of prayer before starting his day at school. A sleepy-looking businesswoman strode to her seat carrying a steaming cup of coffee in one hand and her leather briefcase in the other.

As others continued to arrive, I welcomed the group and led a few minutes of quiet praise to God. Then I passed around our pictorial church directory and asked the group to pray for each person or family picture there.

The prayers were blunt, sincere — and offered in alphabetical order! Soon we were up to the letter "F" in the church directory, and the woman with the coffee cup began to pray, "Heavenly Father, please take care of the Faust family today."

Startled by the sound of my own name, I listened more intently as she prayed for my wife: "Lord, it must be hard to be a minister's wife; help Candy cope with her responsibilities today." Unexpected tears began to burn in my eyes as she prayed for each of our three children by name, and then continued: ". . . and help Dave as he prepares his sermon this week. Give him the strength and wisdom he needs for today. . . . "

Later, after everyone else had gone, I sat quietly in my church office wondering, "Why was I moved so deeply when they prayed for me?" I'm not usually a very emotional person — certainly not quick to tears.

But somehow that little prayer group had hit a nerve.

Suddenly I realized: I could not recall the last time someone in the church had prayed for me by name! It wasn't that my congregation didn't *love* me. They demonstrated consistent care and encouragement in many ways. The problem wasn't even a lack of *prayer* in our church. People were praying a lot, both individually and in groups.

No. The problem, I had to admit, was *me!*

I had become an unsuspecting victim of the lone ranger syndrome.

I had not been *transparent* enough. When was the last time I had *asked* my people to pray for me? They heard my preaching, sought my advice, and respected my leadership. But did they really know me as a *person?*

On the surface, I enjoyed a warm relationship with the congregation. I resisted being placed on a pastoral pedestal. I made myself vulnerable by selectively sharing some of my struggles and using my own humorous goof-ups as sermon illustrations. Yet somehow, I had pulled down the blinds over the window of my heart. Like the lone ranger, I was a masked man.

Another mark of the lone ranger syndrome: I had not been *assertive* enough. Most of the time, it's easier for me to be an encourager than a confronter. I tend to hide my negative feelings rather than share them. Instead of saying "no," "stop," or "I disagree," I compliantly allowed people to manipulate my time and sap my energy. To some, I may have looked like the brave lone ranger riding valiantly into the sunset. But in reality I was walking wounded, suffering in silence. Only my wife knew the real hurts of my heart.

To make matters worse, I had not been *prayerful* enough. My quiet times were short, shallow, and stale. The lone ranger syndrome reaches critical proportions when the victim even feels distant from God.

Since that early-morning prayer meeting nearly five years ago, I have made several small but important changes. Spurred on by my own sense of need, I have learned some ways to overcome the lone ranger syndrome.

Worry-Reducing through Small Group Involvement

Two years ago I joined a *prayer and accountability group.* It is impractical and unwise for ministers to divulge our inmost thoughts indiscriminately to *everyone.* But we must have *someone* — and if we expect our spouses to bear the full brunt of our burdens alone, we make *them* vulnerable to their own lone ranger syndrome.

According to a survey of nearly 1500 church leaders, less than half meet regularly with a prayer partner. Sadly, one out of four do not even feel they have a trusted friend in the ministry.[7] God intends that His people serve Him "shoulder to shoulder" (Zeph 3:9), connected with others in the body of Christ. Too often, however, personal relationships in the church resemble a group of people riding on an elevator: detached, impersonal, they spend a few minutes together with little conversation, and are glad when the doors open so they can get on with their lives.

As Daniel Webster once said, "There are many objects of great value to man which cannot be attained by unconnected individuals, but must be attained, if attained at all, by association."[8]

Long ago, Socrates described the sad condition of the "lone ranger syndrome": "If you asked a man how many sheep he had, he could easily tell you the precise number; whereas he could not name his friends or say how many he had, so slight was the value he put upon them."[9]

Graceful leaders need to experience what David Seamands calls "group grace":

> Many of the worst barriers to God's grace come from the dysgrace of unhealthy and destructive personal relationships in the past. Therefore many of those barriers will *be removed largely through healthy and constructive personal relationships in our present.* This is where *group grace* enters the picture.[10]

The three men who meet with me once a week provide a safe refuge. We are similar in age and spiritual maturity; our personalities blend comfortably; and we trust each other to keep confidences. Importantly, we have no roles to play, and no reasons to impress each other. No masks are needed here. We pray, share our struggles, offer an occasional word of advice, and laugh a lot.

The men in my small group keep me from feeling like a lone ranger. Instead of treating me like a shepherd, they treat me like one of the sheep.

Worry Reducing through Personal Vulnerability

I have also learned to *request specific prayer* more often. A few months ago, our church was facing an important decision. Because our church serves a university community, we needed to rent additional space for our campus ministry. After several months of frustrating work, however, we still had not found the right facility.

In the past I would have brooded and worried privately over such an issue; but this time I decided to share the burden. I approached six young adults in the church and asked them to share with me in one week of focused prayer about our campus ministry location. Soon after our week of prayer, an ideal meeting room became available at a lower cost than we had thought possible — and our shared burden suddenly became a shared joy.

Graceful leaders are *vulnerable* leaders. The word "vulnerable" comes from the Latin *vulnus* which means "wound." To be vulnerable, one must be capable of being wounded. At first, it might seem that vulnerability could create more worry, but actually the opposite is true. As Cecil Osborne explains,

> Much anxiety is generated in the anxious personality by a need to be "guarded." The guarded personality is, consciously or unconsciously, afraid that his secret will be discovered. He spends a vast amount of . . . energy guarding his secret. It may be that he is an angry person and has spent a lifetime pretending to be saccharine sweet, in which case he is usually unaware of the pretense. Or it may be a generalized and largely unconscious fear that other emotions will get out of control. Thus he invests a great deal of energy in maintaining a false front, the pretense that he is not like that at all.[11]

Henri Nouwen is right: the minister must dare to be "the wounded healer."[12]

Worry Reducing Through Shared Leadership

Most important, I am learning to *change my leadership style*. John Donne was right, "no man is an island."[13] No one is big enough to be a whole *continent* either. In God's geography, I am simply one stone which joins with others to form a temple. I have begun leaning more heavily on the team effort of our elders and other staff members instead of trying to handle so many issues alone.

An ancient abbot, Nilus, correctly observed, "He who mixeth with the crowd hath often wounds."[14] But he who tries to stand alone gets hurt too. Sometimes the pain of loneliness is a self-inflicted wound.

We can be strong leaders without being lone rangers.

It is time to dismount from the big white horse and take off our masks.[15]

SUMMARY

Worry is one of the most difficult challenges leaders face, yet even in our anxious moments, God can help us grow gracefully. God "has given us new birth into a living hope through the resurrection of Jesus Christ from the dead" (1 Pet 1:3). To overcome worry, "living hope" must become a practical reality, not a theological abstraction. God's grace enables us to live hopefully, even in times of pain or discouragement.

When others observe my ministry, I want them to see living hope, not constant worry.

I do not want to be a meteorized minister. After all, meteors shine brightly for a few brief moments, then burn out.

NOTES: CHAPTER NINE

[1]See the article on "Meteorizomai" in Gerhard Kittel's *Theological Dictionary of the New Testament*, Vol. IV (Grand Rapids: Eerdmans, 1967), pp. 630-631, and "New Testament Words" by Kenny Boles in the Ozark Bible College *Compass* (July, 1984).

[2]G. Campbell Morgan, *Studies in the Four Gospels*, "Matthew" (Old Tappan, NJ: Fleming H. Revell Company, 1931), p. 68.

[3]Quoted by James Dobson in *What Wives Wish Their Husbands Knew About Women* (Wheaton, IL: Tyndale House Publishers, 1975), p. 42.

[4]Lewis Copeland, ed. *Popular Quotations for All Uses* (Garden City, NY: Garden City Publishing Company, 1942), p. 39.

[5]Archibald Hart, *Unlocking the Mystery of Your Emotions* (Dallas: Word Publishing, 1989), p. 142.

[6]Cited by George Alder in "Overcoming Anxiety," *The Lookout*, July 22, 1984.

[7]H.B. London, Jr., "Pastor to Pastor" (newsletter published by Focus on the Family), October, 1992.

[8]Quoted in *Sky*, August, 1992, p. 14.

[9]Quoted in *Diogenes Laertius*, translated by R.D. Hicks, Vol. I (Cambridge, MA: Harvard University Press, 1966), p. 161.

[10]David A. Seamands, *Healing Grace* (Wheaton, IL: Victor Books, 1988), p. 178.

[11]Cecil Osborne, *Release from Fear and Anxiety* (Waco, TX: Word Publishing, 1976), p. 112.

[12]"On the one hand, no minister can keep his own experience of life hidden from those he wants to help. While a doctor can still be a good doctor even when his private life is severely disrupted, no minister can offer service without a constant and vital acknowledgment of his own experiences. On the other hand, it would be very easy to misuse the concept of the wounded healer by defending a form of spiritual exhibitionism. A minister who talks in the pulpit about his own personal problems is of no help to his congregation, for no suffering human being is helped by someone who tells him that he has the same problems. Remarks such as, 'Don't worry because I suffer from the same depression, confusion and anxiety as you do,' help no one. . . . Open wounds stink and do not heal. Making one's own wounds a source of healing, therefore, does not call for a sharing of superficial personal pains but for a constant willingness to see one's own pain and suffering as rising from the depth of the human condition which all men share." See Henri J.M. Nouwen, *The Wounded Healer* (Garden City, NY: Doubleday, 1979), p. 88.

[13] John Donne, *Devotions*, XVII.

[14]Helen Waddell, translator, *The Desert Fathers* (Ann Arbor, MI: The University of Michigan Press, 1957), p. 66.

[15]See my article, "Overcoming the Lone Ranger Syndrome," *Church Administration*, February, 1994.

10

CHRISTIAN IDREALISM: GRACE TO HANDLE DISAPPOINTMENT

My friend Steve, a surgeon, was teasing me one day about my work as a minister. "It must be nice to serve the Lord all the time," he said, "instead of facing the problems in the real world."

Since I knew he was only teasing, I laughed with Steve and gently reminded him that preachers have to work long hours, pay their bills, and deal with everyday aggravations like everyone else. Nevertheless, my friend was voicing the all-too-common idea that people who take God seriously are somehow out-of-touch with the real world and the not-so-holy struggles of daily life.

Sadly, many people seem to have concluded that heavenly-minded Christians have no understanding of life in the "real world." By their definition, a realist does what it takes to survive without taking spiritual things too seriously. Unlike atheists who think God is unreal, many so-called "realists" simply dismiss God as irrelevant.

What a mistaken idea! From a Biblical point of view, the person who believes and serves God is the true realist! We do not simply invent God, as Freud theorized, to fulfill our wish for a divine father figure.[1] As Francis Schaeffer put it, we worship "the God who is there."[2] Jesus equips us to cope with the real world. He said His disciples "know the truth" which will set us free (John 8:32). "Truth" is just another name for "reality." To deny God is to deny reality. Satan is the truth-twister, the reality-distorter, the "father of lies" (John 8:44).

Thoughtful Christians are reality thinkers. We recognize the problems of the real world, but we also claim by faith the promises of our real God.

To put it another way, Christians ought to be *"idrealists."* I have coined this compound word to show that we need to combine idealism and realism. Christians live in the "now" while we anticipate the "not yet." While a believer's citizenship is in heaven (Phil 3:20), our daily lives on earth should win the respect of outsiders (1 Thess 4:11-12). We are idealistic because we view the future hopefully, but we are also realistic because we view the present honestly.

REALIST OR IDEALIST?

Finding the right balance between realism and idealism is one of the tougher tasks facing the church leader.

Faithless Realism: the Danger of Growing Cynical

In one sense, leaders must always be idealists. Others may not think about the possibilities of kingdom growth, but the graceful leader must dare to dream. In times of doubt, despair, and difficulty, God's leader must uphold and affirm the timeless ideals of faith, hope, and love. One of the indispensable tasks of the leader is to clarify and communicate the ideals of the group. In this way, a leader should never stop being an idealist.

Our ideals will be severely tested, however. When Moses led the people out of Egypt, he saw by faith the Promised Land which lay ahead (Heb 11:24-29), but his ideals were tested by the harsh realities of forty years in the wilderness. After years of strenuous leadership over a rebellious and stubborn people, Moses finally expressed his exasperation to the Lord: "Why have you brought this trouble on your servant? What have I done to displease you that you put the burden of all these people on me?" (Num 11:11).

For years, David knew he was Israel's anointed king. Yet his circumstances were anything but ideal as he suffered mistreatment at the hands of King Saul. It must have been tempting to grow cynical when he ran for his life and even hid in caves. But David refused to give up his ideals. When he was "most low," David cried out to God "Most High" (Ps 57:2).

Laura Vander Veen, a minister's wife, describes the frustration her husband experienced while serving with a small congregation. Despite his hard work, and despite the fact that people seemed to appreciate his ministry, there were few measurable results: no numerical growth, and little evidence of any substantive change in the spiritual condition of the church. The frustration of such a ministry can be captured in what Vander Veen calls "six searing words": *They'll love you, but nothing happens.*[3]

When nothing seems to be happening, we must guard against cynicism. We can become so "realistic" about the problems and limitations of the church, we lose our ideals. This is faithless realism. It results in pessimism and despondency. "The evil man has no future hope" (Prov 24:20).

We live by faith; we die by cynicism.

Foolish Idealism: the Danger of Chasing Fantasies

On the other hand, graceful leaders must be realistic. Unhealthy leaders deny problems and avoid conflict at all costs. It is good to be positive, but negative factors must be acknowledged and confronted. It is good to dream, but dreams must be translated into action. "One who chases fantasies will have his fill of poverty"

(Prov 28:19).

When I was a boy, all I needed was my ballglove, a rubber ball, and the side of our old garage, and I was transformed into a World Series hero. My team always won my imaginary games, although sometimes I let the other team get close just to make it exciting before I struck out the last batter or hit a grand slam home run to win the game. It was fun to pretend.

But in the real world, we do not always win. We sometimes look like fools, not heroes. Life hurts. People disappoint us. Though prayer offers an outlet for our frustrations, it is not just rubbing Aladdin's lamp. Like the wise men, of Christmas fame, we must do more than "wish upon a star," we must follow the light of Christ even when it leads us into the dangerous domain of life's Herods.

Christians do not live in a dream world. Our faith is not an escape from reality, but a confrontation of reality. As Archibald Hart notes,

> Nothing is to be gained by ignoring reality. Deception is the end of all thinking that distorts or denies the realities of life. The danger in teaching people how to think of unlimited possibilities, to use success-generating imagination and obstacle-overcoming visual strategies is that it may create expectations that cannot be fulfilled. If they are tied to reality, these strategies free you. If they are not, you will lose contact with reality and court disaster. This can easily distort the true nature of life. It can lead to a greater sense of failure or repeated frustrations and depression.[4]

Faithful Idrealism: Finding a Healthy Balance

If we are to grow gracefully, we must be idrealists. As the following chart illustrates, we can be realistic without compromising our ideals.

The Right Balance:

Faithless Realism	**Faithful Idrealism**	Foolish Idealism
"The evil man has no future hope" (Prov 24:20)	**"There is surely a future hope for you" (Prov 23:18)**	"One who chases fantasies will have his fill of poverty" (Prov 28:19)
Unhealthy pessimism about problems	**Healthy optimism about problems**	Unhealthy denial of problems
Negative attitude about the future; No solutions, just questions.	**Faithful hope for the future; Biblical solutions to real life questions.**	Empty dreams of the future; Ivory-tower solutions to questions no one is really asking.

IDREALISM IN ACTION

The concept of idrealism can be useful in a number of ways. Leaders need to be idrealistic about people, about the church, and about life itself.

The Leader's Outlook on People

A raw realist might look at a wealthy, conniving businessman like Zacchaeus and assume he could never be brought to repentance. But Jesus saw Zacchaeus' potential and brought him salvation (Luke 19:1-10). On the other hand, it is foolishly idealistic to assume everyone will be equally responsive. Jesus' encounter with the rich young ruler demonstrates the hard reality of rejection (Mark 10:17-25).

Realistically, some people turn up their noses at the gospel; to them, we are "the smell of death." But to others, God's Word is like a breath of fresh air; to them, we are "the fragrance of life" (2 Cor 2:16).

Ministry is people-work. It is not just programs and projects, buildings and budgets. It is not just sermons and well-crafted lesson outlines. It is giving a cup of water in Jesus' name to people who will sometimes hurt and disappoint us.

Ministry is sculpting servants out of rough-cut stones, developing beautiful pictures out of dark-looking negatives. It is the self-righteous ambition of Saul of Tarsus melting into the grace-centered determination of the apostle Paul. It is the boldness of a great leader emerging from the rugged personality of a Galilean fisherman like Peter.

Ministry is the ugly mingled with the beautiful. It is a well-intentioned woman pouring out her expensive perfume while Judas complains (John 12:1-8). It is one thief mocking and insulting Jesus, while another repents and asks, "Jesus, remember me when you come into your kingdom" (Luke 23:39-43). It is Jesus' disciples gathering with Him after His resurrection — some worshipping Him, some still doubting Him (Matt 28:16-17).

The Leader's Outlook on the Church

My brothers loved baseball as much as I did. Together, we turned our lawn into a miniature baseball field. Well-worn basepaths circled the yard, and our daily games created large bare spots for home plate and a pitcher's mound. Many parents might have complained that we ruined the lawn, but instead, my dad often said, "I will have plenty of time to raise grass after I have raised my boys!"

My dad was in the business of growing a family, not just maintaining a lawn. Churches are in the business of growing a family, not keeping up appearances. Sometimes our congregations are less than beautiful, but we can still be positive about them. Just as with adolescent children, a few blemishes are signs of increasing maturity.

Proverbs 14:4 says, "Where there are no oxen, the manger is empty." An empty manger is neat and clean, but where there are no messes, there are also no oxen to do the work. The principle is simple: "No manure, no milk."[5] Many of us would rather avoid the complications of messy stalls, but the problems of a growing church are worth the hassle. As Johnny V. Miller explains:

A thriving ministry has no shortage of messy stalls:
— Smudge marks along the hall leading to the Sunday school classrooms, the result of a growing children's ministry.
— Complaints from old-timers who feel like it's not their church anymore now that so many newcomers have made the church their home.
— Nervous neighbors worried about the teens crowding the church grounds on weeknights. . . .
— Overcrowded parking lots and members upset about parking on the street.
— A shortage of children's workers because classes must divide again. . . .[6]

For ten years, I ministered with South Nassau Christian Church in Long Island, New York. I moved there with a supportive wife, a new baby, a lot of big dreams — and a keen sense of my own inadequacy. Realistically, some folks said South Nassau would never grow; it was a tiny congregation of fifteen to twenty people meeting in a rented building. But many of us saw the potential for growing a church in this heavily populated area.

I will never forget a meeting which took place in my dining room in 1978, during the early months of my ministry. We had located a vacant church building we hoped to purchase, but to do so we needed the approval of the mission board which was assisting our church-planting effort. Our church treasurer planned a strategy for buying the property based on sizeable growth projections. Nervously, we presented the plans to a group of mission trustees seated around my dining room table.

At first, there was a long pause. One of the men finally spoke, and I will never forget his words: "By human standards, this plan seems impossible. But it would be wrong for us not to try!" That is idrealism in action.

The Leader's Outlook on Life

Shadrach, Meshach, and Abednego were idealistic enough to respond to the king's threats without fear; they believed God was able to save them from the fiery furnace. Yet these men were also realistic enough to see that God might not intervene directly to save them from the fire. Either way, they insisted, "we will not serve your gods" (Dan 3:16-18).

Similarly, Jesus taught His disciples to expect trouble in this life, but to persevere with unrelenting cheerfulness because Christ has overcome the world (John 16:33).[7]

Idrealists understand exactly what the apostle Paul means when he writes, "We are hard pressed on every side, but not crushed; perplexed, but not in despair; persecuted, but not abandoned; struck down, but not destroyed" (2 Cor 4:8-9). As Bob Russell writes,

> . . . Paul was thrown into prison, and he converted the jailer. When he was dragged before kings, he turned the palace into a pulpit. When he was put into solitary confinement in prison, he turned the prison into an author's workshop, and he came out of the dungeon with a good share of the New Testament in his hands. He would be knocked down but never knocked out. Every disappointment was a door; every interruption, an opportunity; every frustration, a stimulation.[8]

DEALING WITH THE DISAPPOINTMENTS OF MINISTRY

According to Warren Wiersbe, "The test of a true ministry is not stars, but scars."[9]

The apostle Paul surely would have agreed. He wrote, "I bear on my body the marks of Jesus," but in the next verse prayed, "The grace of our Lord Jesus Christ be with your spirit, brothers" (Gal 6:17-18). Grace equips us to deal with the disappointments of ministry which leave painful scars on leaders and their families.

Many young preachers graduate from Bible college or seminary filled with zeal and idealism, only to suffer intense discouragement a few years later as they encounter the hard realities of ministry in a sin-infested world. Some ministers experience physical problems like those of Timothy, who suffered frequent illnesses and stomach problems (1 Tim 5:23). Others endure the psychological pain of misunderstanding, criticism, or exasperation at the unrepentant and stubborn attitudes of some with whom they work. Even Jesus once sighed in dismay, "O unbelieving generation, how long shall I stay with you? How long shall I put up with you?" (Mark 9:19).

Youthful idealism, combined with an overwhelming sense of the eternal importance of saving souls, creates high expectations that often are not accomplished in the real world. It hurts to see someone you led to Christ falling prey to the cares of the world. It hurts to hear that a couple whose wedding you performed years ago are now involved in a bitter divorce. It hurts to pour your whole heart into building up a congregation, only to see the church torn by internal strife and division. Many capable and well-intentioned leaders bear such scars as these, and struggle to maintain their idealism about church leadership.

Few wounds hurt more intensely than those inflicted by the shattered remnants of a broken dream.

Unresolved Conflict

Conflict is a normal part of life, but many church leaders find conflict resolution one of the most difficult aspects of our work.

According to Genesis chapter 26, Isaac's servants dug a fresh-water well, but some competing herdsmen quarreled about the well and claimed, "The water is ours!" Isaac named that well "Esek" ("dispute"), then moved on and dug another well; but again, his enemies quarreled over the water, so Isaac named this one "Sitnah," which means "opposition." He moved to yet another spot, dug another well, and finally this time, no one quarreled over it. Isaac named this last well "Rehoboth," which means "room," for as he said, "Now the Lord has given us room and we will flourish in the land" (Gen 26:19-22).

Church leadership often resembles Isaac's experience with the wells. Eventually all of us will face some Eseks and Sitnahs, some disputes and opposition. We spend a lot of time and energy digging for fresh water, only to have some bothersome person or problem come along and stop up the well.

How does an "idrealist" deal with conflict? How can we grow gracefully in spite of conflicts which are difficult to resolve? Because we are committed to God's ideals, we must never allow quarrels to prevent us from seeking water. On the other hand, we must also know when it is time to dig in a different spot.

Idrealists *identify* conflicts. In Australia lives an animal called the shingleback skink which has a fat tail shaped like its head. This unique design frustrates potential predators, which cannot decide which end of the skink to attack! Sometimes church conflicts, like the shingleback skink, are difficult to confront because they are many-sided. We are foolish, however, if we stick our heads in the sand and refuse to admit we are up against a skink in the first place! Once the real source of a problem has been identified, the leader can decide whether, and how, to get involved.

Idrealists *address* conflicts. Some conflicts are best avoided altogether, and church leaders are wise to avoid being "triangled" or put in the position of a third party when their efforts are not really necessary in order to resolve the conflict. "He who guards his mouth and his tongue keeps himself from calamity" (Prov 21:23). Nevertheless, some conflicts must be addressed, and when this is the case, we must not be afraid to speak out. As someone has said, "Sometimes silence is golden, but other times it is just yellow." Leaders must be assertive enough to address the Biblical dynamics of any conflict, and to rebuke sin when necessary (Titus 2:15).

Idrealists *accept* conflict. A certain amount of conflict is unresolvable, and even inevitable. Instead of hiding from it or simply becoming depressed by it, we must learn to follow Jesus' instructions about confronting a wayward brother (Matt 18:15-17) and Paul's instructions about dealing with differences of opinion without sacrificing Christian unity (Rom 14:1-15:7).

Undeserved Criticism

Years ago, I heard about a professional hockey goalie who complained, "How would you like a job where, if you make a mistake, a big red light goes on and 18,000 people boo?"

It is not surprising when people criticize us for making mistakes. The more difficult thing to handle, however, is criticism we do *not* deserve.

The apostle Paul faced criticism from many directions. Festus called him a madman (Acts 26:24), and enemies of the church hounded him from place to place (Acts 17:5-13). The most painful attacks, however, came from within the Christian community itself. Some questioned Paul's qualifications as an apostle (1 Cor 9:1-3), others disliked his speaking style (2 Cor 10:10), and still others criticized his emphasis on grace (Gal 5:1-12). Some even tried to cause Paul trouble while he was chained in jail as a prisoner for the sake of Christ (Phil 1:15-18).

But Paul was an idrealist. He realistically acknowledged his own weaknesses and defended himself against unfair attacks, yet he never abandoned the ideals of Christ's calling in his life. Instead of fretting over the motives of others, he rejoiced that Christ was being preached (Phil 1:18). Instead of spending all his time worrying over the critics' opinion of him, Paul focused on pleasing God and fulfilling his ministry (Phil 3:12-14, 1 Thess 2:4-6). "He had a high view of his office, but kept to a low view of himself, the holder of that office."[10] Kenneth Prior correctly states:

> What then, according to Paul, is the way to respond to criticism? We shall, of course, be ready to ask ourselves if there is any justification for it and if we have wronged anyone we shall, like any other Christian, seek their forgiveness. But we must never forget that it is to God that we are ultimately responsible. Nor must we allow ourselves to undervalue the office God has given us. This will be coupled with a humble view of ourselves which attributes our positions, gifts and successes to God's grace.[11]

Unfulfilled Expectations

For several years, I kept two potted plants in my office. One was a living plant with long green leaves. The other looked similar from a distance, but there was one major difference: it was an artificial plant.

Actually, the artificial plant was easier to have around. It required no care, no maintenance, no fuss. The living plant, on the other hand, was a nuisance at times — requiring regular waterings, the occasional removal of a dead or wilted leaf, and even a repotting or two.

Artificial plants are less trouble. As someone has said, "Plastic flowers attract no bugs." Yet, I have always preferred *living* plants. Yes, they require more effort; but they are *alive* and *growing*. Their growth, in fact, is what creates some of the problems.

If we expect to experience no hassles in life, we will definitely be disappointed in a living, growing church. Life and growth require lots of attention, produce changes, and demand hard work. The alternative, however, is to accept the safe but bland artificiality of non-growth. I would rather accept the problems of something real and alive than contend with something stagnant and artificial.

I may never fulfill all of my own expectations in ministry, let alone everyone else's. But I am determined to cling tenaciously to God's ideals as long as He grants me breath. No matter what other disappointments life may bring, there is one expectation which will not go unfulfilled. Someday Jesus will return in clouds of glory, ready to reward His faithful servants (Revelation 22:12).

When I was a child, I can remember riding home in the car at night. I would usually fall asleep in the back seat while my dad drove. Eventually I would feel the car slow down and hear the crunch of the gravel under our tires as we pulled into the driveway. Even if I were awake, I would pretend to be asleep, because I liked what happened next. My dad's strong hands would reach into the back seat and lift me onto his shoulder, then he would carry me up to bed.

Somehow I think it will be a similar thing when a Christian departs from this life. We have trusted our heavenly Father with the journey; we can also trust Him with the journey's end. With strong hands He will lift us close to Himself, and at last we will enter His rest with His warm words of welcome ringing in our ears: "Well done, good and faithful servant. Enter into the joy of your Lord."

SUMMARY

Christians ought to be idrealists who combine idealism with realism. By God's grace, we can accept the reality of disappointment without losing our ideals or our enthusiasm for God's work.

Idrealism sometimes means "toughing it out" during the hard times ministry brings. But in the meantime, "hope does not disappoint us, because God has poured out His love into our hearts by the Holy Spirit, whom He has given us" (Rom 5:5).

True realists live by faith.

NOTES: CHAPTER TEN

[1]Sigmund Freud described this point of view in his book *The Future of an Illusion*. See *The Freud Reader*, Peter Gay, ed. (New York: W.W. Horton & Company, 1989), pp. 703-704.

[2]Francis A. Schaeffer, *The God Who Is There* (Downers Grove, IL: InterVarsity, 1968), p. 48.

[3]Laura Vander Veen, "Six Searing Words," *Perspectives*, September, 1991, p. 19.

[4]Archibald Hart, *The Success Factor* (Pasadena, CA: Fuller Theological Seminary, 1984), p. 37.

[5]Johnny V. Miller, "The Back Page," *Leadership*, Spring, 1992, p. 146.

[6]*Ibid.*

[7]The prophet Habakkuk expressed a similar approach to life (Hab 3:17-18).

[8]Bob Russell, *Take Comfort* (Cincinnati: Standard Publishing, 1991), pp. 78-79.

[9]Warren W. Wiersbe, *Be Encouraged* (Wheaton, IL:Victor Books,1984), p. 164.

[10]Kenneth Prior, *Perils of Leadership* (Downers Grove, IL: InterVarsity, 1990), p. 164.

[11]*Ibid.*, p. 178.

11

THE INSIDE STORY: A GRACEFUL QUEST FOR PERSONAL HOLINESS

When I was in high school, a professional photographer visited our school and took pictures of everyone in my senior class. When the finished portraits came back, my classmates and I were pleased to see that most of us looked better through a camera's lens than we do in real life! Evidently the portraits had been touched up, airbrushing away any unsightly blemishes or uncombed hair.

As far as I know, no one has ever successfully invented a spiritual airbrush. Nevertheless, Christian people often are tempted to show the world a touched-up version of our real selves. Careful not to reveal our spiritual blemishes and imperfections, we can easily fall into a game of unholy charades.

Andre Agassi, the tennis player, used to appear in television commercials in which he advertised a certain brand of cameras with the slogan, "Image is everything." Image, though, is *not* everything. In fact, one's image can actually obscure the things that are most important. The prophet Ezekiel warned about false prophets who covered their flimsy lies with whitewash (Ezek 13:10-16). Jesus compared the hypocrites of His day to dirty dishes which look clean on the outside but are filthy on the inside (Matt 23:25-26). Externalism and lack of authenticity are two of the devil's most potent weapons. Even the most dedicated Christian leader may find himself hounded by hypocrisy, hiding behind a religious façade.

In his poem "The Hollow Men," T. S. Eliot paints a painfully pessimistic picture of religious emptiness. Hollow men, he wrote, speak with voices "quiet and meaningless as dry grass."[1]

The Lord calls us to be *hallowed* men, not hollow men.

He cares about the inside story, the real condition of our inner selves. Others may be impressed by outward appearance, but God looks on the heart. He not only wants us to be productive; He wants us to be holy (1 Thess 4:3). "Make every effort to live in peace with all men and to be holy; without holiness no one will see the Lord" (Heb 12:14).

BEING DIFFERENT, MAKING A DIFFERENCE

Just as the Holy Bible is different from all other books, and the Holy Land is the unique place where God's Son walked the earth, God calls His people to be different. We are a holy people, sanctified not by our own merits but by the grace of God. "It is because of Him that you are in Christ Jesus, who has become for us wisdom from God — that is our righteousness, holiness, and redemption." (1 Cor 1:30). God did not make us holy so we would sit comfortably on a heavenly shelf but so we would "declare the praises of Him who called you out of darkness into His wonderful light" (1 Pet 2:9).

Holy people are called to be different so we can make a difference in God's world.

Authenticity of Holiness

Holiness, then, springs from who we really are, not from what we pretend to be. Artificial holiness is a poor substitute for the real thing. Phoniness steals away our integrity and weakens our influence. The constant prayer of the graceful leader is, "Lord, make me real."

Pretense and artificiality are unnecessary but common burdens. A. W. Tozer wrote:

> There is hardly a man or woman who dares to be just what he or she is without doctoring up the impression. The fear of being found out gnaws like rodents within their hearts. The man of culture is haunted by the fear that he will some day come upon a man more cultured than himself. The learned man fears to meet a man more learned than he. The rich man sweats under the fear that his clothes or his car or his house will sometime be made to look cheap by comparison with those of another rich man.[2]

A minister friend who took his family to Disneyland says, "I always leave Disneyland with the same three impressions: (1) Things appear to be real, but they are not. (2) At times it seems you are part of the action, but you are not. (3) On some rides there seems to be an element of risk, but there is not." It is all too easy to take a Disneyland approach to our faith — to seem real, to seem a part of the action, to talk about taking risks while choosing to play it safe. As my friend says, "Disneyland is a great place to visit, but I don't want to live there."[3]

Ironically, church leaders can become so concerned with the growth of our churches, we neglect our own walk with God. Socrates once told about certain sculptors who go to great lengths to turn a block of marble into the likeness of a man, but neglect their own personal development and end up as mere blocks, not men.[4]

Graceful leaders must be more than mere blocks; we must be genuinely holy. As E. M. Bounds noted, "The church is looking for better methods; God is looking for better men."[5]

Eccentricity of Holiness

Holy people are peculiar people. To update the terminology a bit, we are "eccentric" people. Eccentric means "off center" or having a different center. We Christians unashamedly acknowledge that our lives have a different focal point than they used to have before we accepted Christ. Now our lives are centered on Christ, not self. Our priorities revolve around His will, not our personal desires.

According to pollster George Gallup, "In a typical day the average person stays in front of the TV set nearly twenty-five times longer than in prayer."[6] An article in *Christianity Today* reports that per capita giving for world evangelism has dropped significantly among American Christians. In 1987, for example, Americans spent about the same amount ($1.7 billion) on one brand of video games as we spent on world missions.[7]

Holy people, however, dare to challenge these trends. When we dare to order our lives around a different center, our use of time, money, and energy may indeed seem eccentric to others around us.

The common view of Christians as merely "nice" people is a limp, pale caricature of the tough, dynamic life of discipleship Jesus desires. I do not want my tombstone to read: "David Faust — He Was a Nice Guy." The very word "nice" comes from the Latin *nescius* which originally meant "ignorant," "foolish," or "one who does not know." The Bible challenges us to be committed, to be kind, to be good, to be gracious — but nowhere does it say we should be nice!

Jesus was far more than "nice." At times He displayed a likeable sense of humor, and He offered unparalleled compassion and grace to people around Him. But He was not a bland, harmless fellow who produced warm fuzzy feelings in those around Him. Jesus challenged the status quo; He required dedication, not neutrality.

Jesus' ministry was not dictated by the priorities of others around Him. He was not a slave to the typical rabbinic patterns of His day.

TEN "ECCENTRIC" LESSONS FROM JESUS' MINISTRY

1. Jesus was willing to do dirty work, like washing feet (John 13:1-17).
2. Jesus paid attention to children, even when others tried to shoo them away (Mark 10:13-16).
3. Jesus allowed His emotions to show, including anger (Mark 3:5), love (Mark 10:21), and sorrow (John 11:35).
4. Jesus never attended a board meeting or committee meeting!
5. Jesus associated freely with sinners (Matt 9:10).
6. Jesus recognized and developed potential in unlikely people like lepers and the demon-possessed (Mark 1:40-42, 5:1-20).
7. Jesus talked about the real world, not just the religious world, so that the people "listened to Him with delight" (Mark 12:37).
8. Jesus voluntarily spent time among the sick and the outcasts of society (Matt 4:23-24, John 5:1-15).
9. Jesus dared to do right even when His opponents were ready to criticize Him (Mark 3:1-6).
10. Jesus sometimes chose private prayer over public ministry (Mark 1:35-36, Luke 6:12).

In short, Jesus was holy! He was different. Regardless of the pressures others placed upon Him, He was determined to do the Father's will. Likewise, Jesus calls His followers to the eccentricity of holiness.

Simplicity of Holiness

The Law of Moses contained hundreds of commands, and the Scribes and Pharisees added hundreds more binding traditions of their own (Mark 7:1-13). Jesus' prescription for holiness, by contrast, is remarkably simple — although anything but easy: "Be perfect, therefore, as your Father in heaven is perfect" (Matt 5:48). Indeed, according to Jesus, the whole law could be expressed in two comprehensive commandments: love God and love your neighbor (Matt 22:37-40).

Anyone who honestly strives to fulfill these basic requirements, however, soon realizes how desperately we depend on the grace and power of God to grow in holiness. The American patriot, Benjamin Franklin, described his personal struggle as follows:

> I wish'd to live without committing any fault at any time; I would conquer all that either natural inclination, custom, or company might lead me into. As I knew, or thought I knew, what was right and wrong, I did not see why I might not always do the one and avoid the other. But I soon found I had undertaken a task of more difficulty than I had imagined.[8]

In our own strength, we could never achieve the holiness God requires, but the sanctifying work of the Holy Spirit accomplishes through the Word what we could never do alone (John 17:17, Acts 2:38, Gal 3:2-3, 1 Pet 1:2). By the sacrifice of Jesus on the cross, God "has made perfect forever those who are being made holy" (Heb 10:14). Christ enables us to "put on the new self, created to be like God in true righteousness and holiness" (Eph 4:24).

However well-intentioned their origins, religious rules can never match the holy effectiveness of Christ's finished work. Performance-oriented "do's and don'ts" eventually produce frustration, not freedom. Like a heavy blanket thrown over a glowing fire, legalism suffocates holiness and clouds our vision with unholy smoke.

Alexander Solzhenitsyn, who lived for years under the oppressive communism of the former Soviet Union, once told an audience at Harvard University that "whenever the tissue of life is woven of legalistic relationships, this creates an atmosphere of spiritual mediocrity that paralyzes man's noblest impulses."[9] As the apostle Paul put it, "the letter kills but the Spirit gives life" (2 Cor 3:6).

How easily we are entrapped by the same kind of mistaken reasoning which deceived the Pharisees in Jesus' day. Holy people seem to be the ones who dress right when they go to church, sit on the platform during important conventions, and deliver long and flowery prayers on a moment's notice. Yet Jesus encouraged a simpler approach to holiness. He approved the simple reverence of a widow who gave her donation secretly and sacrificially (Mark 12:41-44), and He commended the quiet loyalty of Mary when she sat listening at His feet (Luke 10:38-42).

If we are to be graceful leaders, we must learn the authenticity, the eccentricity, and the simplicity of holiness.

REAL PEOPLE, REAL FAITH

The Bible tells us about a number of real people who show what it means to be holy. Faithful holiness permeated their everyday lives. We can learn a lot about genuine holiness by considering the examples of these men and women who lived gracefully.

Joseph illustrates *moral purity*. When he was tempted to yield to the seduction of Potiphar's wife, he refused, saying, "How then could I do such a wicked thing and sin against God?" (Gen 39:9).

Sexual temptation is the Achilles' heel which brings down many a church leader. Randy Alcorn warns, "As we more and more hear of Christian leaders succumbing to immorality, we must not say merely, 'There, but for the grace of God, I might have gone,' rather, 'There, but for the grace of God — and but for my alertness and diligence in the spiritual battle — I may *yet* go.'"[10] The daily prayer of a church leader needs to be, "Create in me a pure heart, O God" (Ps 51:10).

Caleb is an example of *courage*. Even as he grew older, Caleb remained strong, vigorous, and unafraid. He told Joshua, "So here I am today, eighty-five years old! I am still as strong today as the day Moses sent me out; I'm just as vigorous to go out to battle now as I was then" (Josh 14:10-11). In fact, Caleb insisted on tackling a tough military assignment: driving the Anakites from their large well-fortified cities. He was successful because of his courage and because he followed the Lord wholeheartedly (Josh 14:12-14). As the Lord told Moses, Caleb was the kind of man who had a "different spirit" (Num 14:24). He had the courage to stand alone, to be different from others around him.

It takes courage to be holy. When leaders act boldly, God's people are energized. When leaders are afraid, God's people are paralyzed and immobilized. Alexander the Great used to terrify his foes by scattering around huge bridle-bits where his enemies could easily find them. His enemies concluded that Alexander's army had huge, super-sized horses. The resulting fear became one of Alexander's most potent weapons.[11]

Similarly, our adversary the devil uses fear to weaken us in our efforts to grow gracefully. The more we cultivate holy fear of our heavenly Father, the less we will cower under the intimidation of real and imaginary foes. "Perfect love drives out fear" (1 John 4:18). Isaiah 8:12-14 urges, "Do not fear what they [unbelievers] fear, . . . The Lord Almighty is the one you are to fear, He is the one you are to dread, and He will be a sanctuary." Peter quotes these Old Testament verses in 1 Peter

3:14-15, but with one important difference. While Isaiah says God will be our sanctuary, Peter says God will establish His sanctuary within His people: "in your hearts set apart Christ as Lord."

A person who exemplified this kind of holy fear was a fellow named *Hananiah*, whose life demonstrated great *reverence* for God. According to Nehemiah 7:2, Hananiah "was a man of integrity and feared God more than most men do." Now there is a beautiful description of a godly leader! Hananiah stood out because he cultivated an unusually intense reverence for the Lord.

Thomas á Kempis was right when he urged that no matter how skilled we may be in the Scriptures or how high our standing in life, we should "be grounded in true humility, and full of divine love," and "be always purely and sincerely seeking God's honor."[12]

A godly woman, *Dorcas*, illustrates another aspect of holiness: *compassion*. According to Acts 9:36, this woman (also known as Tabitha) "was always doing good and helping the poor." With her own hands, she made (and evidently gave away) robes and other garments for people in need. When she died, these handmade blessings formed a cherished legacy of love in the town where she lived. When Peter raised her from the dead, Dorcas' life became an even more impressive testimony to the power and compassion of God (Acts 9:39-42).

True holiness results not in isolation from others but involvement with others. Holiness is not a haloed head but a helping hand. Holiness means sharing money, food, clothes, and shelter, giving with a generous and cheerful attitude. Paul tells us to offer our bodies as "living sacrifices, holy and pleasing to God," then immediately says to use our gifts for the good of Christ's body, the church (Rom 12:1-8). As holy people, we must learn to do useful things with our hands so that we "may have something to share with those in need" (Eph 4:28).

Priscilla and Aquila show that holiness also means *risk-taking.* They dared to invite the eloquent preacher Apollos to their home so they could instruct him more adequately in the way of the Lord (Acts 18:24-28). They risked their safety and comfort by hosting the apostle Paul in their home and working together with him in the tentmaking trade (Acts 18:1-4). They allowed their home to be used as a meeting place for the church, and risked their very lives for the sake of the gospel (Rom 16:3-5).

In *The Pursuit of Holiness,* Jerry Bridges points out that the heroes of faith mentioned in Hebrews chapter eleven (Abel, Noah, Abraham, Moses, and others) were risk-takers because of their faith. According to Bridges, "The holiness described in the Bible calls us to do more than separate ourselves from the moral pollution of the world around us. It calls us to obey God even when that obedience is costly, when it requires deliberate sacrifice and even exposure to danger."[13]

Holiness is not without its risks. Under the Old Testament law, priests were exposed to danger every time they examined lepers who claimed to be cleansed. The priests had to go outside the camp, to the leper colonies, where they were exposed to the physical hazards and social stigmas of contagious leprosy. There the priests examined the lepers' skin and verified their recovery (Lev 14:1-3). Priests had to be risk-takers in order to be God's instruments of healing and cleansing.

Holiness is more than taking the safe road; it is taking the right road whatever the cost. It is daring to walk through dangerous territory with God's help. It is daring to speak up for the truth of God. Anyone who dares to teach or preach the Word can appreciate the kind of holy courage which moved David to pray, "I do not hide your righteousness in my heart; I speak of your faithfulness and salvation. I do not conceal your love and your truth from the great assembly" (Ps 40:10).

Another real person we meet in Scripture, *Timothy*, illustrates the holy quality of *unselfishness*. Paul writes of him, "I have no one else like him, who takes a genuine interest in your welfare. For everyone looks out for his own interests, not those of Jesus Christ" (Phil 2:20-21).

Unselfishness is rare indeed. Rare is the person who truly strives to be Christ-centered rather than self-centered, commitment-conscious rather than comfort-conscious. Rare is the person who consistently thinks of the needs and feelings of others and is concerned mainly for the self-esteem and worth of others instead of his own. Second Timothy 3:1-5 lists about twenty different sins which characterize human behavior in the last days. The first sin mentioned is, "People will be lovers of themselves." No doubt the other sins (lovers of money, proud, abusive, and so on) spring naturally from the polluted wellspring of selfishness.

The Holy Spirit's sanctifying work in the believer leads to an ever-increasing awareness that it is not our own life to live, but Christ's life to be lived through us (Gal 2:20). This is what it means to grow gracefully, and this is what it means to live a balanced life. M. Scott Peck argues:

> All adults who are mentally healthy submit themselves one way or another to something higher than themselves . . . .[14]

Our choice is to live according to either Philippians *1:21* ("For to me, to live is Christ and to die is gain") or Philippians *2:21* ("For everyone looks out for his own interests, not those of Jesus Christ").[15]

OBEDIENT CHILDREN, NOBLE MEN

The graceful leader models obedience to Christ. First Peter 1:14-16 urges, "As obedient children, do not conform to the evil desires you had when you lived in ignorance. But just as He who called you is holy, so be holy in all you do; for it is written: 'Be holy, because I am holy.'"

Similarly, Jesus used children to illustrate the quality of character He desires in kingdom people. "Let the little children come to me, and do not hinder them, for the kingdom belongs to such as these" (Mark 10:14).

What is it about children which the Lord wants to see in all of us? Many answers have been given. Children tend to be trusting. There is a purity and innocence about them. They are often satisfied with simple things. They tend to be pliable, teachable, moldable. They are filled with potential. But Jesus emphasized one trait above all others: Children are *receptive*. "Anyone who will not receive the kingdom of God like a little child will never enter it" (Mark 10:15).

Graceful leaders are those who, like little children, realize their dependence on the heavenly Father. Our holiness is received, not achieved. Our position of holiness is a gift from God; our growth in holiness is a continuing process which requires our compliance and effort as obedient children. Thus Peter can speak of our sanctification as both a *position* — we are "a holy nation" (1 Pet 2:9) — and a *process* — we ought to "live holy and godly lives" and "grow in the grace and knowledge of our Lord and Savior Jesus Christ" (2 Pet 3:11,18).

When obedient children mature, they become noble adults. According to Isaiah 32:8, "the noble man makes noble plans, and by noble deeds he stands."

To be graceful leaders, we must be *noble people*,

exemplifying the kind of inner holiness God desires. We must make *noble plans*, boldly striving to accomplish God's will. We must perform noble deeds, putting faith into action.

SUMMARY

Integrity, holiness, spiritual maturity — these are the marks of a graceful leader.

Others may be impressed by outward appearance, but God looks on the heart. He cares about the inside story, the real condition of our inner selves. The Lord wants us to be productive, but outward productivity is no substitute for genuine spiritual growth.

Scripture calls us to develop balanced, holy lives in which we work out our own salvation with fear and trembling, while at the same time recognizing it is God who works in us to do His good pleasure (Phil 2:12-13). To become graceful leaders, we must "purify ourselves from everything that contaminates body and spirit, perfecting holiness out of reverence for God" (2 Cor 7:1).

NOTES: CHAPTER ELEVEN

[1]T.S. Eliot, *The Complete Poems and Plays, 1909-1950* (New York: Harcourt, Brace, and World, Inc., 1952), p. 56.

[2]A.W. Tozer, *The Pursuit of God* (Harrisburg, PA: Christian Publications, 1948), p. 114.

[3]Rick Rusaw, "From the Heart," First Christian Church, Longmont, CO (July. 1992), p. 4.

[4]Quoted in *Diogenes Laertius*, translated by R.D. Hicks, Vol. I (Cambridge, MA: Harvard University Press, 1966), p. 165.

[5]E.M. Bounds, *Power through Prayer* (Grand Rapids: Baker Book House, 1977), p. 5.

[6]George Gallup, Jr., and George O'Connell, *Who Do Americans Say That I Am?* (Philadelphia: Westminster Press, 1986), p. 89.

[7]"New Figures Show Per Member Giving Drop," *Christianity Today*,

March 19, 1990, p. 48.

[8]John Bigelow, ed., *The Autobiography of Franklin* (Philadelphia: J.B. Lippincott & Co., 1868), pp. 213-214.

[9]Quoted by George Alder in "The Letter Kills," *The Lookout*, August 19, 1979, p. 15.

[10]Randy C. Alcorn, "Strategies to Keep from Falling," *Sins of the Body*, Terry C. Muck, ed. (Dallas: Word Publishing, 1989), p. 118.

[11]J.I. Packer, Merrill C. Tenney, and William White, Jr., eds. *The World of the New Testament* (Nashville: Thomas Nelson, 1982), p. 41.

[12]Thomas á Kempis, *Of the Imitation of Christ*, (Chicago: Donohue Brothers, n.d.), p. 80.

[13]Jerry Bridges, *The Pursuit of Holiness* (Colorado Springs: NavPress, 1978), p. 139.

[14]M. Scott Peck, *People of the Lie* (New York: Simon and Schuster, 1983), p. 78.

[15]Warren W. Wiersbe, *Be Joyful* (Wheaton, IL: Victor Books, 1978), p. 72.

12
QUIET AMBITION

Mention the word "ambition," and many of us immediately think of high stress and high achievement. We
usually associate ambition with the desire for rank,
fame, prestige, power, or advancement. The Latin *ambi-
tio*, from which the word is derived, literally meant
"going around" or "go-getting." As we might say today,
an ambitious person is a real "go-getter." The ancient
Romans used this term to describe the way a candidate
for public office would go around trying to get people to
vote for him. For most of us, the word ambition sounds
like hard-driving activity and pressure to perform.

How odd it seems, therefore, to find the apostle Paul
urging Christians, "Make it your ambition to lead a
quiet life, to mind your own business and to work with
your hands . . . " (1 Thess 4:11). Make it your ambition
to lead a quiet life! This colorful verse could be translated, "Make it your ambition to have no ambition," or
"Seek restlessly to be still."[1]

The Greek word *philotimeomai* (translated "make it
your ambition") comes from a compound of *philos*
(kindly disposed, friendly toward) plus *timao* (to honor
or revere, to set a high price or value on something).
According to Leon Morris, this word signifies "a whole-
hearted and energetic pursuit of the object."[2] The word
appears only two other times in the New Testament:

Romans 15:20 — "It has always been my ambition to
preach the gospel where Christ was not known . . ."
(NIV). [The New American Standard Bible translates, "I

aspired to preach . . ."]

2 Corinthians 5:9 — "So we make it our goal to please Him . . ." (NIV). [The King James Version translates, "Wherefore we *labor* . . ."]

Just as our goal must be to preach the gospel and to please God, the goal of graceful leaders must also be to lead a quiet life. Selfish ambition is the enemy of quiet ambition. Richard John Neuhaus warns that personal ambition is an enemy of ministers from which we should "draw back as from lethal poison."[3]

There is such a thing as godly ambition, however, found in the quiet orderliness of a peaceful life which includes ample time for physical labor and personal solitude. We are to "do nothing out of selfish ambition" (Phil 2:3), but if we are to live balanced lives, we must do lots of things out of *quiet* ambition.

A QUIET LIFE

Graceful leaders must develop an action plan for personal growth which includes ample time for inactivity, quietness, and reflection. Well-balanced lives are directed by the Spirit and will of God, not by a drivenness which originates with one's own desire to impress others or even to impress oneself.

The Worry, Sorry and Hurry Factors

We are victims not only of the *worry* factor (discussed in a previous chapter), but also the *sorry* factor (dealing with guilt feelings which occur when we do not accomplish everything we want to do or feel we ought to do). Fortunately, "love covers over a multitude of sins" (1 Pet 4:8). God's love is vast enough, His grace plentiful enough, to cover both the sins we commit and the sins we omit. He does not treat us as our sins deserve. We can only overcome the sorry factor through casting ourselves completely on the mercy of our graceful God. "If anybody does sin, we have one who speaks to the Father in our defense — Jesus Christ, the Righteous One. He is the atoning sacrifice for our sins" (1 John 2:1-2).

For many of us, however, the biggest struggle for balance does not have to do with the worry factor or the sorry factor (guilt). We struggle most of all with the *hurry* factor. Our ambition is not quiet ambition, but the ambition of a fast-paced, high-stress race to accomplish everything we can as quickly as we can.

During a winter snowstorm, I noticed how eagerly my neighbors and I listened to the radio to hear whether our meetings and other activities had been cancelled. I wondered, "If we are so relieved when they are cancelled and we are granted a free evening at home, did we really need to schedule so many activities in the first place?"

As Eugene Peterson has noted, "the word busy is the symptom not of commitment but of betrayal."[4] We are busy, Peterson argues, because we are vain and because we are lazy:

> . . . I want to appear important. Significant. What better way than to be busy? The incredible hours, the crowded schedule, and the heavy demands on my time are proof to myself — and to all who will notice — that I am important. . . .
>
> . . . I live in a society in which crowded schedules and harassed conditions are evidence of importance. I want to be important, so I develop a crowded schedule and harassed conditions. When others notice, they acknowledge my significance and my vanity is fed. The busier I am, the more important I am.
>
> The other reason I become busy is that I am lazy. I indolently let other people decide what I will do instead

of resolutely deciding myself. . . . Anything remotely religious or somehow well-intentioned can be properly assigned to the pastor.

Because these assignments to pastoral service are made sincerely, I lazily go along with them. It takes effort to refuse, and there's always the danger that the refusal will be interpreted as a rebuff, a betrayal of religion and a calloused disregard for people in need.[5]

In my own life, I have struggled earnestly to win the struggle with hurry-sickness. Peterson's questions prick my conscience:

How can I lead people into the quiet place beside the still waters if I am in perpetual motion? How can I convincingly persuade a person to live by faith and not by works if I have to constantly juggle my schedule to make everything fit into place?[6]

The words of Isaiah speak directly to my heart:

In repentance and rest is your salvation,
in quietness and trust is your strength,
but you would have none of it.
You said, 'No, we will flee on horses.'
Therefore your pursuers will be swift. . . .

Yet the Lord longs to be gracious to you;
He rises to show you compassion.
For the Lord is a God of justice.
Blessed are all who wait for Him! (Isa 30:15b-18).

A BALANCED LIFE

Geologists speak of a phenomenon known as "isostasy," an equilibrium maintained within the crust of the earth. "Isostasy" means "equal standing." When an imbalance occurs, earthquakes and volcanic eruptions are the result.[7]

A balanced life results in what we might call "spiritual isostasy," a godly equilibrium which helps prevent spiritual earthquakes. The apostle Paul's prescription for spiritual isostasy includes: minding your own business, working with your hands, winning the respect of outsiders (1 Thess 4:11).

What else needs to be included in an action plan for balanced living? How can church leaders overcome the hurry factory and live a balanced life? Here are some suggestions:

Action Plan for Self

1. *Redefine success.* Self-evaluation should focus more on God's grace and less on society's standards or even our own perfectionistic goals.
2. *Recognize and cease some of the unnecessary activities associated with our drivenness.* For me, this has meant drastically reducing the number of outside speaking engagements I will accept, since these are not at the heart of what I believe God wants me to do with my time.
3. *Develop a theology and strategy of rest.* Many ministers have never really studied the topic of rest, although the Bible has a lot to say on the subject. Most of us simply need to go to bed earlier.
4. *Reduce the hurry factor in our daily lives.* Even little things can help: choosing to talk, eat, and drive more slowly, avoiding the tendency to do two or three things at once. Despite certain extra-busy periods, a weekly work schedule of about fifty-five hours per week seems like a safer "speed limit" than seventy or eighty!
5. *Develop assertiveness skills.* Learn to say "no."
6. *Clarify goals and priorities.* Instead of moving along haphazardly, I want to focus my time and energy on a few important priorities which include ample time for my family and my personal walk with God.
7. *Plan more time for creative work and hobbies.* I am learning that, in balance, such activities as sports, gardening, and creative writing are excellent ways to

use my time. I am also learning to guard my vacation
times more carefully.

8. *Distinguish between the prompting of God and the
promptings of our own insecurity and drivenness.* It is
easy to confuse the two.

9. *Make changes in the way we preach and teach.* I am
trying to develop a more grace-based approach to
proclaiming the good news. As I interact with others,
I want to teach and model personal wholeness and
growth in grace.

Action Plan for the Family

1. *Slow down our pace.* We are learning to spend more
evenings at home, and more Saturdays and Sunday
afternoons doing nothing but resting and having fun.

2. *Spend more time meeting our spouse's needs and
strengthening our marriage.* For us, a workable
approach is simply to schedule once-a-month dates
and at least one special weekend trip per year when
we can get away by ourselves.

3. *Share burdens with others, especially a small prayer
group, and stop bringing so many of the burdens home.*

Longlasting joy and satisfaction in ministry require
that we develop and follow an action plan for dealing
with stress. Our lives and schedules must not be dictated by the worry factor, the sorry factor, and the
hurry factor, but by the grace of God.

A GRACEFUL LIFE

Graceful living means unrelenting discipleship and
loyalty to Christ. Jesus said, "If anyone would come
after me, he must deny himself and take up his cross
daily and follow me" (Luke 9:23). He also warned that
this is a lifelong commitment: "No one who puts his
hand to the plow and looks back is fit for service in the
kingdom of God" (Luke 9:62).

Graceful living means clinging to the cross, and it means finishing the race.

Clinging to the Cross

Several years ago, my congregation decided to paint our church building. Volunteers spent many hours scraping and painting the old wooden shingles. During the summer months, I would occasionally end my office work in the late afternoon and spend an hour or two painting before going home.

One sunny afternoon, despite the fact that I am somewhat uncomfortable with heights, I decided to paint the church's bell tower and steeple. Everything went well at first. Working all alone high on the ladder, I enjoyed the fresh air and exercise as I began to paint the old wooden cross which was nailed to the very top of the steeple. Soon, however, I looked down — and I was startled to see how high I was from the ground. In reality, it was probably only about thirty feet. But from my precarious vantage point, it may as well have been three hundred feet!

Instinctively, I grabbed the wooden cross and held it tightly until the momentary feeling of panic subsided and I carefully made my way down the ladder and onto solid ground. A friend and I eventually finished painting the steeple, but I will never forget the sensation of hanging on to that old wooden cross as if my life depended on it.

In a sense, that incident serves as a parable of life for many of us. We toil busily along, climbing steadily and occasionally enjoying the view from atop the ladder of success. Then suddenly, something reminds us how fragile and risky life really is. For a moment, we think we will fall. Such times are useful reminders that we must cling to the cross! In reality, the cross has always been our only lasting source of security, strength, and success.

Finishing the Race

As the apostle Paul neared the end of his life and ministry, he said, "I have fought the good fight, I have finished the race, I have kept the faith" (2 Tim 4:7). Often the race we run in life does not feel like a short sprint, but a marathon. In some ways it is like a demolition derby in which the object is simply to remain running at the end.

Finishing the race, though, is more than just surviving. It is a noble objective which provides joy and a sense of meaningfulness through all the difficulties of life. "Do you not know that in a race all the runners run, but only one gets the prize? Run in such a way as to get the prize" (1 Cor 9:24).

Those who do not accept God's grace live busy but hopeless lives. Some of the ancient Romans expressed their pagan pessimism with epitaphs engraved on their tombstones which read: "I was not, I am not, I care not."[8] The graceful leader, however, always possesses the quiet ambition which springs from a heavenly hope. We will not quit, nor will we lose hope, for God's grace sustains us as we run the race.

During the 1992 Summer Olympics, one of the competitors in the 800 meter run injured his leg, but he kept running. Despite intense pain, he continued moving toward the finish line — his tear-stained face twisted in agony and disappointment. The crowd cheered, applauding his courageous effort even though the race was already lost.

Finally a man came out of the stands, put his arm around the limping runner, and helped him on to the finish line. Later, reporters explained that the man who came down out of the stands to help was the injured runner's *father*. His dad said, "We started this thing together. We had to finish it together."

Life's race is sometimes painful. But we can make it

to the finish line with our heavenly Father's help.

"He who began a good work in you will carry it on to completion until the day of Christ Jesus" (Phil 1:6).

SUMMARY

"Make it your ambition to lead a quiet life" (1 Thess 4:11). Even busy leaders are called to be still in the presence of God. Our life's ambition must not be to make a name for ourselves, but to magnify His name. "Not to us, O Lord, not to us but to your name be the glory, because of your love and faithfulness" (Ps 115:1).

Graceful leaders must establish an orderly, well-balanced, peaceful approach to life. Not only will this prevent burnout; it will also enable us to provide longer-lasting and more fruitful service to the glory of God.

If our ambition is to grow gracefully, God will provide the resources. We must cling to the cross and continue to run the race.

And we must pray with the apostle John, "The grace of the Lord Jesus be with God's people. Amen."

NOTES: CHAPTER TWELVE

[1]Leon Morris, *The Epistles of Paul to the Thessalonians* (Grand Rapids: Eerdmans, 1976), p. 81.

[2]*Ibid.*

[3]Richard John Neuhaus, *Freedom for Ministry* (Grand Rapids: Eerdmans, 1992), p. 238.

[4]Eugene H. Peterson, "The Unbusy Pastor," *Leadership*, Summer, 1981, p. 70.

[5]*Ibid.*

[6]*Ibid.*

[7]Jean Norton, "Earth: The Scriptural Design" (*Moody Monthly*, April, 1980), p. 79.

[8]Wayne A. Meeks, *The First Urban Christians* (New Haven, CT: Yale University Press, 1983), p. 181.

APPENDIXES

APPENDIX ONE
CLEAR OR CONFUSING?

Graceful churches send messages that are clear, not confusing. They set an atmosphere of understanding and grace, not quarrelsomeness.

2 TIMOTHY 2:15-26

SOURCES OF CONFUSION	RESULTS OF CONFUSION	ALTERNATIVES TO CONFUSION
Quarreling about words	No value; ruins those who listen	Be an unashamed workman who correctly handles the word of truth
Godless chatter	More and more ungodliness; teaching will spread like gangrene; destruction of faith	Stand on God's solid foundation
Foolish and stupid arguments	Quarrels	Be kind, able to teach, not resentful

APPENDIX TWO
GROWTH: A NEW TESTAMENT WORD STUDY

A careful word study reveals that the New Testament does not restrict the concept of growth either to numerical growth or spiritual/maturational growth. Indeed, Scripture uses a variety of terms to describe many different forms of growth.

A. The ordinary word for growth in the Greek New Testament is *auxesis* (growth, increase) or its verb forms *auxano* and *auxo* (to grow, cause to grow, to increase). These words are used to describe various kinds of growth, including the following:

1. *PLANTS* WHICH GROW IN SIZE

   a. Matthew 6:28 — "See how the lilies of the field *grow*."
   b. Mark 4:8 — the seed that fell on good soil "*grew* and produced a crop."
   c. Luke 13:19 — the mustard seed "*grew*, became a tree, and the birds of the air perched in its branches." (Compare Matthew 13:32.)

2. *CHILDREN* WHO GROW IN STATURE

   a. Luke 1:80 — when John the Baptist was small, "the child *grew* and became strong in spirit."
   b. Luke 2:40 — Jesus "*grew* and became strong."

3. *INDIVIDUAL BELIEVERS* WHO GROW IN SPIRITUAL MATURITY

   a. 2 Corinthians 9:10 — God "will *enlarge* the

harvest of your righteousness."

 b. 2 Corinthians 10:15 — "as your faith continues to *grow*."

 c. Colossians 1:10 — "*growing* in the knowledge of God."

4. *THE WORD OF GOD* WHICH GROWS IN INFLU-ENCE

 a. Acts 6:7 — "So the word of God *spread*."

 b. 1 Corinthians 3:6 — "I planted the seed, Apollos watered it, but God made it *grow*."

 c. Colossians 1:6 — "All over the world this gospel is producing fruit and *growing*, just as it has been doing among you since the day you heard it and understood God's grace in all its truth."

5. *THE BODY OF CHRIST* AS A WHOLE WHICH GROWS IN SIZE AND STRENGTH

 a. Ephesians 2:21 — In Christ "the whole building is joined together and *rises* to become a holy temple in the Lord."

 b. Ephesians 4:16 — the body of Christ "*grows* and builds itself up in love, as each part does its work."

 c. Colossians 2:19 — the body grows "as God causes it to *grow*."

B. Another important term is the verb *plethuno* (to increase or multiply), used in passages such as the following:

1. AS A DESCRIPTION OF ABUNDANT NUMERICAL GROWTH:

 a. Acts 6:1 — "In those days when the number of disciples was *increasing* . . . ."

 b. Acts 6:7 — "the number of disciples in Jerusalem *increased* rapidly."

c. Acts 9:31 — the church "was strengthened; and encouraged by the Holy Spirit, it *grew* in numbers, living in the fear of the Lord."

2. AS A DESCRIPTION OF ABUNDANT SPIRITUAL BLESSING:

    a. Acts 12:24 — "But the word of God continued to *increase* and spread."

    b. 1 Peter 1:2 — "Grace and peace be yours in *abundance*." (Compare II Peter 2:2.)

    c. Jude 2 — "Mercy, peace and love be yours in *abundance*."

C. Still another growth-related New Testament term is *prostithemi* (to add). This word is used both of numerical church growth, and of other kinds of blessings which the Lord "adds to" His people:

1. GOD'S PROVISION FOR THE BELIEVER

    a. Matthew 6:33 — "But seek first His kingdom and His righteousness, and all these things will be *given* to you as well."

    b. Luke 12:31 — "But seek His kingdom, and these things will be *given* to you as well."

    c. Luke 17:5 — "The apostles said to the Lord, '*increase* our faith!'"

2. GOD'S ADDITION OF PEOPLE TO THE CHURCH

    a. Acts 2:41 — "Those who accepted his message were baptized, and about three thousand were *added* to their number that day."

    b. Acts 2:47 — "And the Lord *added* to their number daily those who were being saved."

    c. Acts 5:14 — "Nevertheless, more and more men and women believed in the Lord and were *added* to their number."

APPENDIX THREE
COUPLES IN MINISTRY:
SOME BIBLICAL INSIGHTS

A. MR. AND MRS. AQUILA

    1. They endured persecution together. They were forced to leave Rome and move to Corinth because of Claudius' edict against the Jews (Acts 18:1-3).

    2. They were hospitable. They encouraged Paul to stay and work with them in the tentmaking trade. They hosted church gatherings in their home (Acts 18:1-3, Rom 16:3-5).

    3. They were able to teach. They opened their home to Apollos, and opened up the way of God more adequately to this gifted preacher (Acts 18:26).

    4. They were hard workers. They risked their lives for the sake of Paul and the gospel (Rom 16:3-5).

B. MR. AND MRS. APOSTLES

    1. The apostles took their wives along on their missionary travels (1 Cor 9:5).

    2. Peter wrote from experience as a married man when he urged husbands to "be considerate as you live with your wives" (1 Pet 3:7, compare Mark 1:29-31).

C. MR. AND MRS. ELDERS

    1. Overseers (elders) must manage their own families well as evidence of their ability to take care of God's church (1 Tim 3:4-5).

2. Overseers must be "the husband of but one wife" (Greek: "one-woman man"), whose children are "not open to the charge of being wild and disobedient" (Titus 1:6).

D. MR. AND MRS. DEACONS

1. Those who serve as deacons must exemplify proven character ("must first be tested" — perhaps evaluated, as with the elders, in part by their ability to manage their home life in a positive and godly manner (1 Tim 3:8-10).
2. Deacons' wives must be "women worthy of respect, not malicious talkers but temperate and trustworthy in everything" (1 Tim 3:11). (Some believe this refers to deaconesses rather than deacons' wives.)

BIBLIOGRAPHY

BOOKS

Abraham, William J. *The Logic of Evangelism*. Grand Rapids: Eerdmans, 1989.

Alcorn, Randy. "Strategies to Keep from Falling." In *Sins of the Body*, ed. Terry C. Muck. Dallas: Word Publishing, 1989.

Aldrich, Joseph C. *Life-Style Evangelism*. Portland, OR: Multnomah, 1981.

Barna, George. *The Frog in the Kettle*. Ventura, CA: Regal Books, 1990.

_____. *The Power of Vision*. Ventura, CA: Regal Books, 1992.

Barth, Karl. *The Word of God and the Word of Man*. Translated by Douglas Horton. Grand Rapids: Zondervan, 1935.

Bigelow, John, ed. *The Autobiography of Franklin*. Philadelphia: J. B. Lippincott & Co., 1868.

Bounds, E. M. *Power through Prayer*. Grand Rapids: Baker, 1977.

Bridges, Jerry. *The Pursuit of Holiness*. Colorado Springs: NavPress, 1978.

Bruce, F. F. *The Epistle to the Hebrews*. Grand Rapids: Eerdmans, 1964.

Conn, Harvie M. *Evangelism: Doing Justice and Preaching Grace.* Grand Rapids: Zondervan, 1982.

Cook, William H. *Success, Motivation, and the Scriptures.* Nashville: Broadman, 1974.

Copeland, Lewis, ed. *Popular Quotations for All Uses.* Garden City, NY: Garden City Publishing Company, 1942.

Cottrell, Jack. *God the Redeemer.* Joplin, MO: College Press, 1987.

Dawson, John. *Taking Our Cities for God.* Lake Mary, FL: Creation House, 1989.

Dobson, James. *What Wives Wish Their Husbands Knew About Women.* Wheaton, IL: Tyndale House, 1975.

Dodds, E. R. *Pagan and Christian in an Age of Anxiety.* New York: W. W. Norton & Company, 1965.

Eliot, T. S. *The Complete Poems and Plays, 1909-1950.* New York: Harcourt, Brace, and World, Inc., 1952.

Ellis, Joe S. *The Church on Purpose.* Cincinnati: Standard Publishing, 1982.

——————. *The Church on Target.* Cincinnati: Standard Publishing, 1986.

Enroth, Ronald. *Churches That Abuse.* Grand Rapids: Zondervan, 1992.

Foster, Richard. *Celebration of Discipline.* San Francisco: Harper & Row, 1978.

Freud, Sigmund. *The Freud Reader.* Edited by Peter Gay. New York: W. W. Horton & Company, 1989.

Gallup, George Jr., and George O'Connell; *Who Do Americans Say That I Am?* Philadelphia: Westminster Press, 1986.

Hart, Archibald D. *The Success Factor*. Pasadena, CA: Fuller Theological Seminary, 1984.

_____. *Unlocking the Mystery of Your Emotions*. Dallas: Word Publishing, 1989.

Hicks, R. D., translator. *Diogenes Laertius*, Vol. I. Cambridge, MA: Harvard University Press, 1966.

Hiebert, E. Edmond. *Titus and Philemon*. Chicago: Moody Press, 1957.

Hunter, George G. *The Contagious Congregation*. Nashville: Abingdon, 1979.

Hybels, Bill and Lynne. *Fit to Be Tied*. Grand Rapids: Zondervan, 1991.

Johnson, David, and Jeff VanVonderen. *The Subtle Power of Spiritual Abuse*. Minneapolis: Bethany House, 1991.

Johnson, Paul. *A History of Christianity*. New York: Atheneum, 1980.

Lewis, C. S. *Letters to Malcolm: Chiefly on Prayer*. New York: Harcourt Brace Jonovich, 1963.

_____. *Mere Christianity*. New York: MacMillan, 1952.

McGarvey, J. W. *Acts of Apostles*, Vol. I. Cincinnati: Standard Publishing, n.d.

McGavran, Donald A. *Momentous Decisions in Missions Today*. Grand Rapids: Baker, 1984.

Mead, Frank S. *Handbook of Denominations in the United States*, 5th edition. Nashville: Abingdon, 1970.

Meeks, Wayne A. *The First Urban Christians*. New Haven, CT: Yale University Press, 1983.

Morgan, G. Campbell. *Studies in the Four Gospels*. Old Tappan, NJ: Fleming H. Revell Company, 1931.

Morris, Leon. *The Epistles of Paul to the Thessalonians*. Grand Rapids: Eerdmans, 1976.

Neuhaus, Richard John. *Freedom for Ministry*. Grand Rapids: Eerdmans, 1992.

Newbigin, Lesslie. *The Gospel in a Pluralist Society*. Grand Rapids: Eerdmans, 1989.

Norheim, Karen. *Mrs. Preacher: Succeeding as a Minister's Wife*. Joplin, MO: College Press, 1985.

Nouwen, Henri J. M. *The Wounded Healer*. Garden City, NY: Doubleday, 1979.

Osborne, Cecil. *Release from Fear and Anxiety*. Waco, TX: Word Publishing, 1976.

Packer, J. I., Merrill C. Tenney, and William White, Jr., eds. *The World of the New Testament*. Nashville: Thomas Nelson, 1982.

Peck, M. Scott. *People of the Lie*. New York: Simon and Schuster, 1983.

Peters, George W. *A Theology of Church Growth*. Grand Rapids: Zondervan, 1981.

Prior, Kenneth. *Perils of Leadership*. Downers Grove, IL: InterVarsity, 1990.

Rosten, Leo, ed. *Religions of America: Ferment and Faith in an Age of Crisis*. New York: Simon and Schuster, 1975.

Russell, Bob. *Take Comfort*. Cincinnati: Standard Publishing, 1991.

Schaeffer, Francis A. *The God Who Is There*. Downers Grove, IL: InterVarsity, 1968.

Schaller, Lyle E. *Growing Plans*. Nashville: Abingdon, 1983.

Schroeder, Charles R. *The Human Body: Its Structure and Function*. Dubuque, IA: Wm. C. Brown Co., 1971.

Seamands, David A. *Healing Grace*. Wheaton, IL: Victor Books, 1988.

Senter, Ruth. *The Guilt-Free Book for Pastor's Wives*. Wheaton, IL: Victor Books, 1990.

Shenk, David W., and Ervin R. Stutzman, *Creating Communities of the Kingdom*. Scottdale, PA: Herald Press, 1988.

Smith, Kenton K., ed. *Mark*. Cincinnati: Standard Publishing, 1968.

Thomas á Kempis. *Of the Imitation of Christ*. Chicago: Donohue Brothers, n.d.

Tozer, A. W. *The Pursuit of God*. Harrisburg, PA: Christian Publications, 1948.

Waddell, Helen, translator. *The Desert Fathers*. Ann Arbor, MI: The University of Michigan Press, 1957.

Wagner, C. Peter. *Your Church Can Grow*. Ventura, CA: Regal Books, 1976.

Wiersbe, Warren W. *Be Encouraged*. Wheaton, IL: Victor Books, 1984.

_____ . *Be Joyful*. Wheaton, IL: Victor Books, 1978.

ARTICLES IN PERIODICALS

Alder, George. "Overcoming Anxiety." *The Lookout*, July 22, 1984, p. 7.

_____. "The Letter Kills." *The Lookout*, August 19, 1979, p. 15.

"City Gropes in Dark." *The New York Times*, November 10, 1965, p. 1.

Drucker, Peter. "Managing to Minister." *Leadership*, Spring, 1989, p. 20.

Faust, David. "Calling in Reverse." *Christian Standard*, October 17, 1982.

Goetz, David. "Is the Pastor's Family Safe at Home?" *Leadership*, Fall, 1992, p. 39.

Guinness, Os. "Church Growth — Weaknesses to Watch." *Tabletalk*, February, 1992, p. 52.

_____. "The Cult of Relevance and the Management of Need." *Tabletalk*, June 1992, p. 50.

Gulbranson, Jorie. "What Every Pastor's Wife Wants from Her Husband." *Leadership*, Fall, 1992, p. 24.

"The Guide." Published by Grand Canyon National Park, Vol. XV, Number 6, June 28-August 11, 1992, p. 11.

Hart, Archibald D. "The Loss-Proneness of Ministry." *Minister's Personal Library Journal*, 1981, p. 3.

Kehl, D. G. "Burnout: The Risk of Reaching too High." *Christianity Today*, November 20, 1981, p. 26.

Leo, John. "The Warm Success of Dr. Hug." *Time*, November 15, 1982.

London, H. B., Jr. "Pastor to Pastor." *Focus on the Family Newsletter*, October, 1992.

Lucado, Max. "The Applause of Heaven and Earth." *Leadership*, Summer, 1992, p. 19.

Miller, Johnny V. "The Back Page." *Leadership*, Spring, 1992, p. 146.

"Mt. Rushmore Gets Long-Delayed Dedication." *The Cincinnati Enquirer*, July 4, 1991.

New Figures Show Per Member Giving Drop." *Christianity Today*, March 19, 1990, p. 48.

Norton, Jean. "Earth: The Scriptural Design." *Moody Monthly*, April 1980, p. 79.

Palmer, Earl. "Evangelism Takes Time." *Leadership*, Spring, 1984, p. 23.

Peterson, Eugene. "The Pastor's Sabbath." *Leadership*, Spring, 1985, pp. 53-54.

_____. "The Unbusy Pastor." *Leadership*, Summer, 1981, p. 70.

Rusaw, Rick. "From the Heart." Newsletter of First Christian Church, Longmont, CO, July, 1992, p. 4.

Vander Veen, Laura. "Six Searing Words." *Perspectives*, September, 1991, p. 19.

Woods, Robert M. "Church Growthism: The New Heresy?" *The Restoration Herald*, July, 1992, p. 8.

LECTURES

Brown, Nathan. "Social Networks and Burnout." Fuller Theological Seminary, April 29, 1992.

Dobson, James. "What Wives Wish Their Husbands Knew About Women." Focus on the Family Radio Broadcast, June 1, 1992.

Hart, Archibald D. "The Minister and Anger." Fuller Theological Seminary, April 30, 1992.

ABOUT THE AUTHOR

David Faust grew up on a farm near Hillsboro, Ohio. He attended New York Christian Institute, earned degrees from Empire State College (B.A.), Kentucky Christian College (M.Min.), Cincinnati Bible Seminary (M.A., M.Div.), and Fuller Theological Seminary (D.Min.).

While in college, David served as a team member with Christ In Youth, Inc. He has served in preaching ministries for two years with the Hickory Lane Church of Christ in Washington Court House, Ohio, and for ten years with the South Nassau Christian Church in Baldwin, New York. In 1989, he helped to plant the congregation where he now serves as part-time minister, University Christian Church in Cincinnati.

He has served full-time on the faculty of Cincinnati Bible College since 1988, teaching Bible and ministry courses. In 1989, David was the recipient of the excellence in teaching award presented by the Greater Cincinnati Consortium of Colleges and Universities.

Among other current projects, David is a contributing writer for a new NIV study Bible to be published by Zondervan and Christianity Today. He has authored or co-authored two books of puppet plays, numerous articles, songs, and study materials, and created cartoons published by *Leadership* journal.

David and his wife Candy have been married for eighteen years, and are the parents of three children: Matthew, Michele, and Melinda.

ENDORSEMENTS

"Through the concept of truly grace-filled relationships, David Faust makes the prospect of Christian leadership not only possible but exhilarating. He offers real help for Churches and their leaders to develop genuinely constructive partnerships in place of the stress and conflict so often found in this association. The result can be a climate of grace-in-action that fosters healthy growth of the church and in the personal lives of its members."

Joe Ellis
Church Growth Consultant
Author: *The Church on Purpose*

"This book addresses the issues raised by church growth with keen pastoral discernment. Its publication provides a timely ministry to those leaders who are struggling with the challenge to grow a church, and now feel more intimidated than inspired by the insights they have received through reading the literature and attending the seminars."

Eddie Gibbs, professor
Fuller Theological Seminary
Author: *I Believe in Church Growth*

"What a wonderful book! Dave Faust communicates with clarity and passion the need for balanced churches and church leaders. I found his book very helpful for my personal life and as a ministerial resource."

Bob Russell, minister
Southeast Christian Church
Louisville, Kentucky

"I believe that the book addresses a very critical issue in church leadership today. 'Unbalanced living' seems to be a central theme in much ministry. This book offers very practical and down to earth help for how an intense church leader can grow both professionally and personally. The book covers critical issues and is an important counterbalance for many contemporary distorted views of leadership."

Archibald Hart, Dean
Graduate School of Psychology
Fuller Theological Seminary